SPENCER & CYNDI NORDYKE

—

LIVING THE FILLIONAIRE LIFE

FOREWORD BY PASTOR GEORGE PEARSONS

Living the Fillionaire Life
by Spencer & Cyndy Nordyke

Published by Blaze Publishing House
www.blazepublishinghouse.com
info@blazepublishinghouse.com

A complete list of Bible translations used in this book are located in the back of the book. Please refer to this list for any/all Bible translation abbreviations, copyrights, and publishing information.

Manuscript Development | Kent Booth
Cover Design | Ryan Nordyke
Photographs of Spencer & Cyndy | Katelyn Holm (katelynholm.com)
Prepared for Publication | Ministry Solutions, LLC
Interior Design & Pagination | Laura-Lee Booth

ISBN-13: 978-1-8833442-00-2

To

Pastors George and Terri Pearsons

Thank you for being our lifetime friends.

We're so thankful to God that He had us

get ordained together.

Thank you for being our pastors, for loving us,

for believing in us, and sparking our faith

to reach into the realms of the impossible

for such a time as this.

CONTENTS

Foreword
by Pastor George Pearsons

S pencer asked if I would write a foreword for his book, and I told him I would be honored to. But, commitments and demands kept getting in the way of fulfilling my assignment.

It had been a very busy season for us. My wife and I were traveling, preaching, leading our church, and doing a lot of "life." I finally blocked out some time on a Sunday afternoon following church. That long day began at 4:30 a.m., and we had a service to attend that evening. So, wearily, I went up to my office, pulled out his manuscript, and began reading.

Something supernatural happened.

The more I read this book, the more energized I became. I woke up!

Page after page, it was talking directly to me. In a short period of time, my faith was "shaken AND stirred," and I found myself thrilled at the prospect of *Living the Fillionaire Life!*

I got so excited about what I read; I kept saying, "I need to read this again and again—OUT LOUD!"

Spencer Nordyke has been an inspiration to me for many years. I have always marveled at his preaching. He has a way of looking at life on a much higher plane.

He is an "out-of-the-universe" thinker. When he and Cyndy attend church, it is a blast to call on him to give a word. We all know it will be something we had never considered.

And *that* is what this book is all about:

GOING WHERE YOU'VE NEVER GONE BEFORE!

It will literally stretch your faith and enlarge your capacity to believe God for all He desires for you to do and have. Get ready for limitations to be removed and your mind to be renewed to a new, fresh, and exciting way of thinking.

So, if you will excuse me, I am going to read this book again . . . and again . . . and again!

Pastor George Pearsons
Eagle Mountain International Church at Kenneth Copeland Ministries
Fort Worth, Texas

Introduction

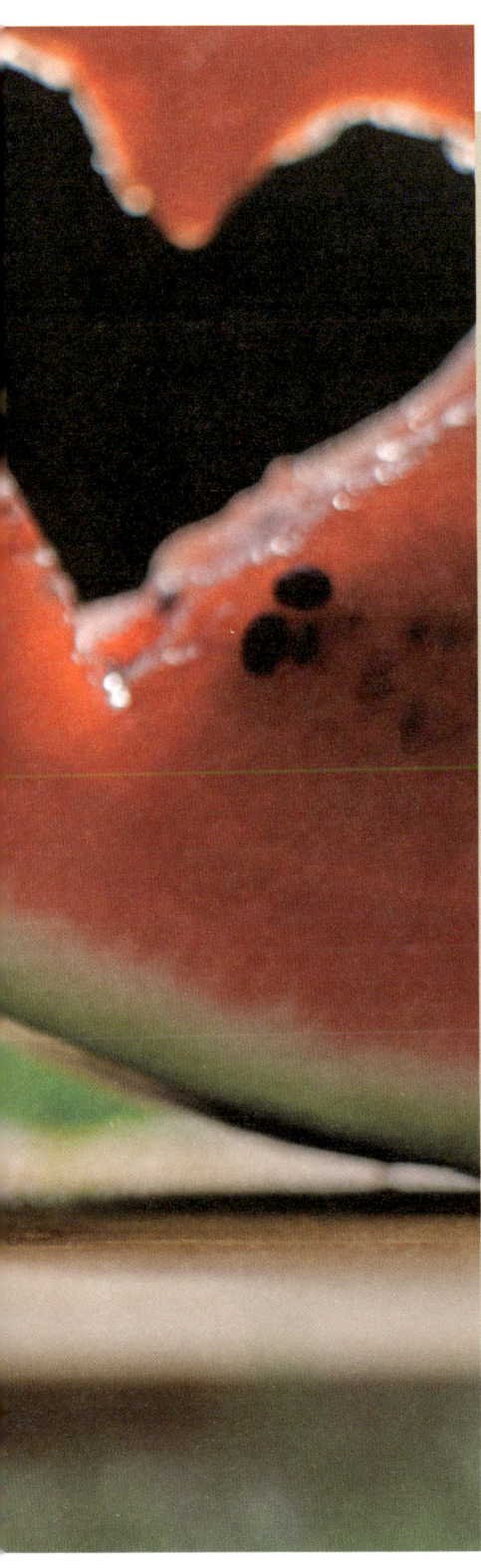

Have you ever been hungry? Not the late afternoon, in-between-meals-snack kind of hungry; I'm talking about where your stomach felt like it was about to touch your spinal cord. That feeling is not fun, but there's something even worse . . . being hungry and having no money!

Been there, done that.

When I was seventeen years old, I left Michigan and migrated over a thousand miles south to attend college. For the first time in my life, I was totally on my own—no friends, no family, no car, and barely any money. Ah, the glory days of college!

Thankfully, I quickly landed a job as a life guard at a local swimming pool. The job was great, but with no car I had to find a means of transportation. So, I bought a bike. It wasn't fancy; but, hey, it got the job done.

HUNGRY
| hun • gry |

HAVING AN EAGER DESIRE, REQUIRING SUBSTANCE TO ENRICH ITSELF.

Most of my classes were in the morning, so I was able to work about thirty hours a week. Practically all the money I earned went to pay my school bill, which also included housing. I was so thankful to have the opportunity to be in college, have a place to live, have a job, and have a means of transportation—sort of!

College was a great learning experience, but it didn't take long to figure out there were some things I had to learn on my own.

It's called growing up!

Paying my school bill first left me with about five dollars to buy food for the week. That's right—a whopping five bucks. Needless to say, I became quite financially creative at a very young age. To give you an idea, here is a sample of my five-dollar shopping list for a week's worth of food:

* 1 box of oatmeal

* 1 loaf of bread

* 1 jar of peanut butter

* 5 pot pies (the store brand ones that cost twenty-five cents)

oto credit: Dano via Visualhunt.com

An average daily menu looked something like this:

Breakfast: oatmeal with a little bit of sugar on it—that was, if I had any.

Lunch: a peanut butter sand-wich. (No, not peanut butter *and jelly*, because I usually didn't have any!)

Dinner: a pot pie (If you're trying to figure out what that is, Google® it! You'll be glad you did.) My favorite was chicken pot pie; it so reminded me of chicken soup—my favorite comfort food.

During those days, I only weighed about a hundred and thirty pounds soaking wet, which isn't very much for a guy who is five-foot, eleven-inches tall and wears a size twelve shoe. But the good news was, I was making it and wasn't starving.

Five dollars wasn't much, but sometimes I could stretch it out, especially if my friends invited me over for a meal. Sadly, that didn't happen very often.

Being only seventeen and completely on my own, I had many weeks where there were more days than food! It was in those times that I would go on what I called an "involuntary fast!"

I experienced more than my fair share of them.

Manna from Heaven

One day I was completely out of food, so I decided to take a walk and clear my mind a bit. I've always had a pioneering and adventurous spirit about me, so this was a perfect time to take off and find new places to explore. Yes, I was hungry . . . and broke!

While walking through a field close to my apartment complex, I literally stumbled upon a ripe watermelon about the size of a football. Who knew that water-melons grew right by my house? Well, they normally didn't, but this one did!

Can you guess what a hungry college student does when he finds a watermelon laying on the ground? You're exactly right! I broke that baby open and devoured the whole thing—bit by bit and piece by piece. Watermelon juice dripped all down my face, but I didn't care. I was in the wilderness; God had provided manna, . . . and I received!

But that wasn't all.

The secret of spiritual success is a hunger that persists. It is an awful condition to be satisfied with one's spiritual attainments. God was and is looking for hungry, thirsty people.

| Smith Wigglesworth |

Blessed are those who hunger and thirst for righteousness for they shall be filled.

Matthew 5:6 (NIV)

As I got up to leave, there lay yet another big, plump, juicy watermelon. Wow! A double blessing! I picked it up and went straight to a friend's house to share. Of course, you might be asking, "Why didn't you take it home for the next day?" Good question. Maybe in my "faith rush" I thought if God could make watermelons appear today, who knows what might appear tomorrow? I figured He guided my footsteps; and if I kept on praising Him, He'd show me more of His goodness.

Whenever I think about this story, it reminds me of a scripture found in Isaiah:

> *"Come, all you who are thirsty, come to the waters; and you who have no money, come, buy and eat!"*
> **Isaiah 55:1 (NIV)**

It's one thing to be hungry—in the natural—but there's a totally different type of hunger that far exceeds the need for food: It's a spiritual hunger that can only be filled by the Spirit of God.

I don't know about you, but I firmly believe the Body of Christ is coming into a brand new awakening! We're moving up to a new level of faith in God, where we simply ask and receive without any doubts, delays, or disappointments!

* Ask and receive.

* No doubts.

* No delays.

* No disappointments.

It really boils down to this simple question: Do you really believe God or not? Think about the things God has promised. He said:

* He would provide.

* We are more than conquerors through Him who loved us.

* He has forgiven all our sins and healed all our diseases.

. . . just to name a few.

● ● ● ● ● ● ● ● ● ● ●

"COME, ALL YOU WHO ARE THIRSTY, COME TO THE WATERS; AND YOU WHO HAVE NO MONEY, COME, BUY, AND EAT!"

ISAIAH 55:1A (NIV)

● ● ● ● ● ● ● ● ● ● ●

GOD CANNOT LIE. GOD ONLY SPEAKS THE TRUTH. GOD SAID IT. GOD MEANT IT. GOD EXPECTS US TO HONOR HIM BY BELIEVING WHAT HE SAYS!

One of God's most amazing desires is for His children to learn to live in abundance. Now, you might say, "But I don't have any money!" That's okay. You won't need it! You have His Word. He is God. He provides, blesses, and sends provision and healing to anyone who will say, "Yes, I receive it!"

And it all starts by being hungry!

Stretch it Out

As you read this book, let your faith expand. It's time to stretch your faith to believe more than you've ever believed. I'm talking about a faith that sees everything God has promised, with:

* NO more choke points.

* NO more limitations.

* NO more excuses.

Do you think this way of life is beyond you? Think again! This is the "normal" Christian life, and it's well within your reach. As a matter of fact, this new level of living has its own name. Keep reading, and you'll learn all about it.

Are you thirsty? Then come to the waters and drink. Are you hungry? Come, buy, and eat—even without any money. Get ready to become all that God wants you to be!

CHAPTER 1

*I Need a
New Word*

I love to pray!

I love to spend time with God!

I love to help people!

I love that God is a God of creativity, and His desire is for us to be creative!

I am a seer. One of the qualities of this gift is the ability to see things differently than others. Therefore, I'm always asking God to help me see the *new* thing! My desire is to see like God sees, especially when it comes to what He wants to do in the spirit realm. I feed that creativity in prayer, stretching myself so I can see things in a fresh way. It's not always easy. God always keeps me on my toes. Sometimes it's fun. Sometimes it's encouraging. Sometimes He's correcting my thinking. Whatever the case, my prayer time always helps me to wrap my faith around what God wants to do in my life.

Not only am I a seer, I'm also a dreamer. Ever since my college days, I've carried big dreams in my heart. One day not long ago, while in a time of prayer, I told the Lord that it would be great if He made me a millionaire. Then I could do all these things that were in my heart. His response was very direct and a bit shocking: "NO!"

"No?" I replied, "What do You mean, 'No?'"

And then I heard Him speak in my spirit, "Why would you limit Me to that?"

"Okay, then, how about a billionaire?"

"That's still a measure. Don't limit Me to natural measures."

It didn't take long to see the error of my ways. My thinking needed a drastic change. I was looking at natural limitations which were keeping me from experiencing all God wanted to do for me.

I, then, cried out in desperation, "Lord, I need a new word and a new vocabulary to communicate Your unlimited power in my prayers!"

As I began to pray in the Spirit, a very simple and powerful word floated up into my mind:

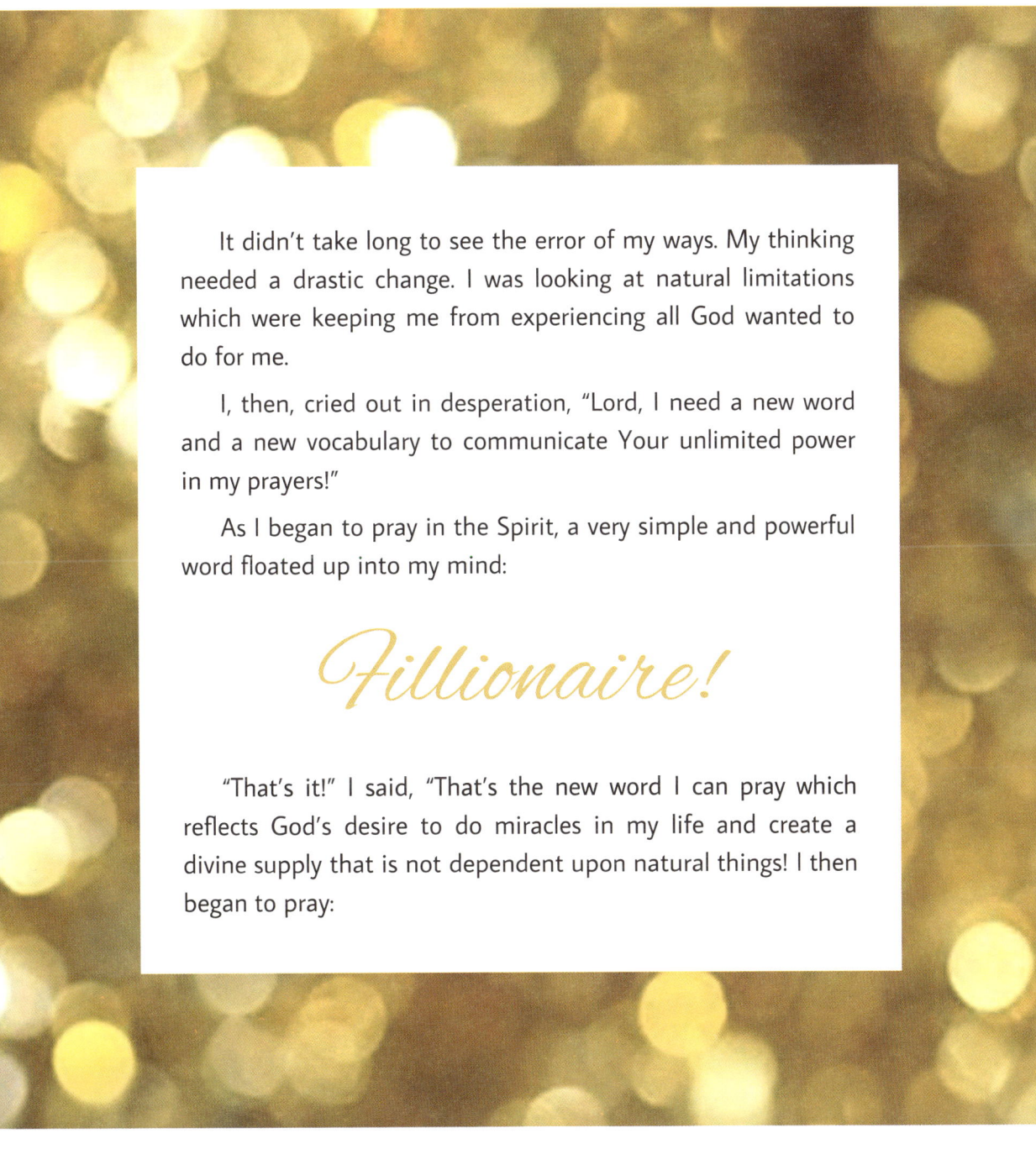

Fillionaire!

"That's it!" I said, "That's the new word I can pray which reflects God's desire to do miracles in my life and create a divine supply that is not dependent upon natural things! I then began to pray:

CREATIVE

| cre • a • tive |

HAVING THE POWER TO CREATE, EXERTING THE ART OF CREATION.

"Lord, please make me a FILLION-AIRE; so wherever I go, I can believe You to pour out Your miracle-working power until every need is met and every person is healed and filled with Your goodness!"

That prayer was just the beginning of an incredible journey.

Since the word "FILLIONAIRE" isn't in the dictionary, I thought I'd look up the root word "fill." What came to my attention was that this word is both a noun and a verb. By definition, it means:

"an amount of something that is as much as one wants or can bear; to occupy to full capacity; to supply to an extreme degree; up to the max."

Take a minute and examine these. Now, think about your own life. Are you living the FILLIONAIRE life? A life filled to full capacity? One that has an extreme degree of supply? If not, then hang on! You're about to rise to FILLIONAIRE status!

The "Original" Fillionaire

As I began to pray this out and study the Word, I quickly realized there was someone who had already lived the FILLIONAIRE life on this earth. His name is Jesus!

Jesus lived and operated in all the fullness of God. God used Him to heal every disease and meet every need until there was nothing missing or broken. Everywhere Jesus went, everything was filled with God. He was the original FILLIONAIRE!

Jesus' "FILLIONAIRE FLOW" (as I like to call it) started at the very beginning of His ministry. After being baptized by John in the Jordan River, Jesus continued to follow the leading of His Father out into the wilderness, where He overcame the devil. Soon, the time would come to reveal His FILLIONAIRE status— at a wedding.

The stage was set. Jesus was in attendance by divine appointment. Mary, His mother, would be the catalyst. (It's awesome how God regularly uses moms as a catalyst.) At twelve years old, Mary had told her son that it wasn't His time; but now at thirty, she would line every detail up for His first miracle.

The wedding was well under way. Everyone was having a great time. Suddenly, the entire celebration was in jeopardy of being ruined by one element: a shortage. Mary quickly told her son, "They have no wine." (See John 2:3.) Jesus, then, echoed what His mother had spoken to Him eighteen years earlier: "My hour has not yet come." Mary didn't even respond to that. Instead, she told the catering staff, "Whatever He says to you, do it!"

Think about all the responses Jesus could have given. He could've said, "Here's some money; go buy some more wine," or, "I know a guy who makes wine; here's his address." Maybe, "There's some wine at our house. Go get it and bring it to the feast." Any of these would have

been an appropriate reply, but none of them were on Jesus' mind. Instead, He gave this directive:

"FILL THE HUGE WATER POTS WITH WATER."

Notice the first word out of His mouth: "Fill!"

This was the beginning of Jesus' miracle ministry.

The servants did what He said and then came back for further instructions. Jesus then said, "Take some to the host." When the host tasted what came out of the water pots, He was amazed. It was the finest wine of the entire night! He then asked the groom, "Why did you save the best for last?"

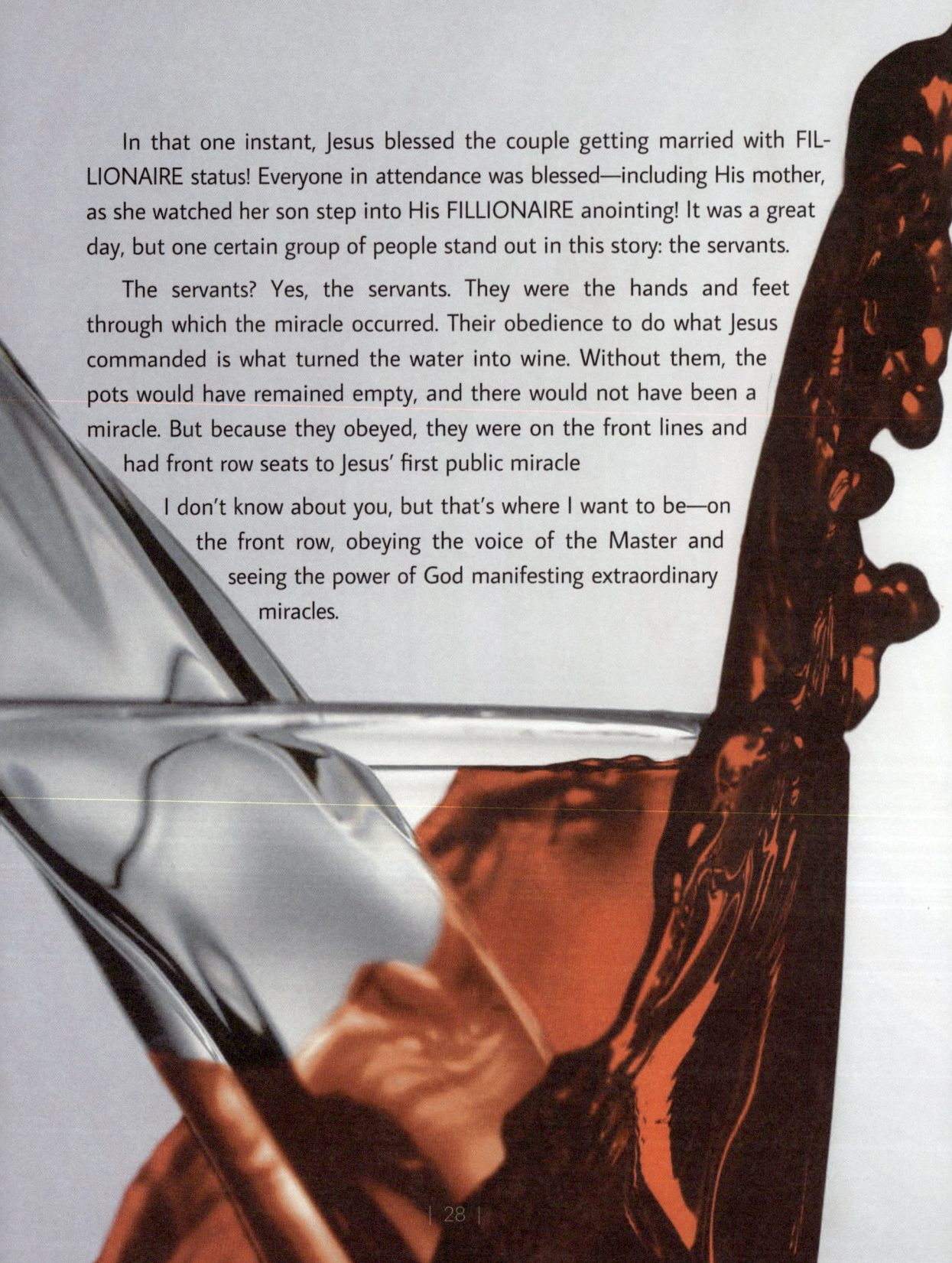

In that one instant, Jesus blessed the couple getting married with FIL-LIONAIRE status! Everyone in attendance was blessed—including His mother, as she watched her son step into His FILLIONAIRE anointing! It was a great day, but one certain group of people stand out in this story: the servants.

The servants? Yes, the servants. They were the hands and feet through which the miracle occurred. Their obedience to do what Jesus commanded is what turned the water into wine. Without them, the pots would have remained empty, and there would not have been a miracle. But because they obeyed, they were on the front lines and had front row seats to Jesus' first public miracle

I don't know about you, but that's where I want to be—on the front row, obeying the voice of the Master and seeing the power of God manifesting extraordinary miracles.

Where There's a Need . . .

Whatever Jesus does, you can be guaranteed it's the best! When you think about that, you realize that all our feeble efforts to accomplish things on our own—instead of receiving a miracle from Him—seem ridiculous. We all have needs. That's inevitable. But when there's a need, it simply means there's room for a miracle!

Go back to the wedding. There was Jesus, a regular attender who was having a great time, minding His own business. Suddenly, a need arose: They ran out of wine. Not only did a need arise that day, but Jesus arose . . . and filled it! And here's good news: God hasn't run out of miracle power!

He's willing and able to fill every need we could ever encounter.

God's people need miracles!

The church needs miracles!

This generation needs miracles!

As we serve Him and follow His leading, we will see miracles before our very eyes, coming from our willing hands.

Let these same words Mary told the servants ring in your spirit:

"WHATEVER HE SAYS TO YOU, DO IT!"

Imagination is everything; it's the preview of life's coming attractions.

| Albert Einstein |

"I Want My Church Back!"

It was a bright and sunny Sunday morning. Cyndy and I were in town, so we drove out to our home church, Eagle Mountain International Church, just north of Fort Worth, TX. What started as a fairly normal Sunday was about to take a one-hundred-and-eighty-degree turn.

Little did we know that years of prophecies spoken were about to be fulfilled.

It is about a forty-five-minute drive from our house to the church, and we usually spend that time praying for the service, for Pastors George and Terri Pearsons, and for the church in general. We always pray however God leads us.

We arrived shortly before the service began. As the music started, everything "seemed" pretty normal, except there was an underlying expectancy that something special was about to happen—something unusual, something supernatural.

When Pastor George took the platform, he told the congregation how the Lord had visited him the day before. He went on to share what the Lord had spoken to his heart:

● ● ● ● ● ● ● ● ● ● ● ●

"Every prophecy that the Lord has given Kenneth Copeland Ministries and Eagle Mountain International Church is coming to pass NOW!"

● ● ● ● ● ● ● ● ● ● ● ●

"... When there's a need, it simply means there's room for a MIRACLE!"

"WELCOME TO THE REVIVAL CAPITAL OF THE WORLD!"

The very instant he released those words into the atmosphere, there was an explosion in the spirit realm. A release came from Heaven, and the room erupted with praise. He shared some of the specific prophetic words God had given to the church over the years. Then he left the platform and went into the audience, praying for people in need of healing and miracles.

People were being touched and blessed. The Spirit of the Lord was present to heal. It was like time stood still. Before we knew it, it was the middle of the afternoon. Yet, no one noticed that four or five hours had already passed. Miracles were

Imitate God, since you are the children He loves.

Ephesians 5:1
| God's Word Translation |

breaking out everywhere. Jesus was being a FILLIONAIRE! He was filling us all up; and, once again, He had saved the best for last!

Our church has not been the same since that moment. Services continue to randomly break out in the direction of prayer and healing. As a result, people from all over the world have come for ministry.

One major thing that the Lord told Pastor George stood out in my spirit. He said, "I want My Church back . . . filled with signs, wonders, miracles, and all the gifts of the Spirit in operation." Listen to the cry of the Lord:

"I WANT MY CHURCH BACK . . . FILLED!"

This isn't just the mandate for our church; it's the cry of the Lord for His Church worldwide—and it's happening all around the world.

More and more, the Spirit of God is completely taking over our services and pouring out miracles. It's not just for the "elect." This outpouring is for every church and every pastor who will allow Him to move. God is hungry to be our God.

The question is: are we hungry for Him? Do we desire to see the glory of God manifest in our places of worship like never before?

Do we want to be like Jesus—FILLIONAIRES? That's what Jesus was! He was a FILLIONAIRE, filled with the anointing and power. Not only was He the "New Wine"; He was filled with the new wine!

The choice is ours.

God has an unlimited supply of love, ability, resources, answers, miracles, and healing. The Bible says to simply ask, and you will receive miracles. Seek Him, and you will find miracles. Knock and miracle doors will fly open.

It's time we realize that Jesus is our example. It's time to be like our Master.

It's time to live . . .

THE FILLIONAIRE LIFE!

Fillionaire
STRATEGIES
#1

...FOR LIVING THE FILLIONAIRE LIFE!

* Decide to start living the FILLIONAIRE life!
* Boldly ask God for miracles.
* Feed your spirit by meditating on a miracle from the Bible daily.
* Ask God for more creativity.
* Pray and stretch yourself to see things differently.

DECLARE THESE:

"I am stepping into the FILLIONAIRE life."

"For it was the Father's good pleasure for all the fullness to dwell in Him." (Colossians 1:19, NASB)

"I boldly ask You, God, for miracles!"

"... They spoke boldly about the Lord, who confirmed their message about his good will by having them perform miracles and do amazing things." (Acts 14:3, GW)

"I feed my spirit miracle food from Your Word!"

"Then those men, when they had seen the miracle that Jesus performed, said, 'This is truly that prophet that should come into the world.'" (John 6:14, WEB)

"I ask You, God, for more creativity in my faith!"

"You see that his faith and his actions were working together, and his faith was made complete by what he did." (James 2:22, NIV)

"I stretch my faith to see things differently!"

"And as He was praying, the appearance of His face changed, and His clothes became radiantly white." (Luke 9:29, BSB)

• • • • • • • • • • • • • • •

CHAPTER 2

*Don't Budget
Your Miracles*

It's interesting how God loves to speak to me on my way to church. One Sunday while driving, I was praying for the service, as usual, suddenly I heard these words in my spirit:

DON'T BUDGET YOUR MIRACLES!

I had to stop and think about that one for a moment! What was God saying? Then, it dawned on me. When it comes to miracles, many people have this mentality: "God, if You will give me just one miracle, I will never ask for another as long as I live!" As if God only has a limited supply of miracle power.

After hearing what the Lord said, I set my heart to pray and meditate on this thought. What exactly does it mean to not budget God's miracles? Every day I meditate on this because, believe me, I'm believing God for an abundance of miracles. One thing I've come to realize is this:

BUDGETS LIVE IN OUR WORLD BUT NOT GOD'S.

Budgets are only necessary when there's a limited supply. If you're on a fixed income or a salary, you budget your money accordingly. If you over extend yourself, then you wind up with more month than money! Time is another item you budget. There's a limited supply of hours in a day—twenty-four to be exact—so you budget your time to do everything you need to do within that space.

UNLIKE OUR NATURAL WORLD OF LIMITATIONS, GOD'S MIRACLE-WORKING POWER IS UNLIMITED.

There's no rationing or shortage of miracles in the mind of God. He never runs out! Thus, we don't have to budget how many times God can supernaturally work on our behalf. He never budgets miracles . . .

. . . and neither should we!

In studying the ministry of Jesus, I began to see how He healed the multitudes of people for days without ever running out of miracles. For example, in Matthew Chapter 14, Jesus was on a multi-day ministry adventure. Miracles were flowing. People were getting healed and delivered. One day, everyone in the crowd was hungry. But, did Jesus take a break? No, just the opposite. He miraculously fed five thousand men, plus women and children— quite possibly over twenty thousand people.

And how did He do it? With only five loaves of bread and two fish.

But that was just the beginning.

Then, after everyone was fed, He instructed His disciples to gather the fragments that remained, which equaled twelve baskets *full* of food.

Many times I've wondered why there were twelve baskets left over, then I realized there were twelve disciples doing the gathering. When they had FILLED their baskets, the multiplication stopped. If there had been seventy disciples, they would have filled up seventy baskets. One hundred and twenty disciples would have produced one hundred and twenty baskets, and so on. In other words, the supply would have continued until all the people and the baskets were *full* with fish and bread.

Not half full, but totally FILLED!

That same Jesus is still in the miracle working business today. What miracles do you need? Many times when we hear the word "miracle" we automatically think of desperation. But your miracle might be some dreams in your heart which at the moment seem impossible to obtain. Broaden your horizon. God is not limited when it comes to miracles. Tap into His unlimited supply.

Take a moment and list the top five miracles you need right now:

1. _____

2. _____

3. _____

4. _____

5. _____

You prepare a table before me in the presence of my enemies. You anoint my head with oil. My [brimming] cup runs over.

Psalms 23:5
| Amplified Classic Edition |

Whatever you're facing today, whatever miracle you need Jesus to do for you, rest assured that God's miracle supply does not stop until you have all that you need and more. His desire is for your life to be overflowing with more than enough!

Why?

So you can share and give to others.

• • • • • • • • • • • •

I CALL IT THE MIRACLE FLOW! MIRACLES FLOW *TO* YOU, SO THEY CAN FLOW *THROUGH* YOU.

• • • • • • • • • • • •

The Miracle Flow

One of the greatest joys in life is giving and being able to help other people. I call it the miracle flow! Miracles flow *to* you, so they can flow *through* you. You have to start where you are with what you have. Practice receiving miracles from your Heavenly Father. Then, make it a habit to give to others.

Having a great sense of God's love for us and those around us positions us to experience more displays of His miracle power. With an unlimited supply of the goodness of God, all things are possible.

Cyndy and I have practiced this principle for years. Remember the bicycle I rode to work in college? I gave it to someone; and God gave me a car! That was just the beginning.

Over the years, we have given several cars away to other people. There's something astounding about giving someone a car, mainly because you become God's instrument of miracle provision. Your obedience becomes someone's miracle testimony!

It's called living in the miracle flow.

Not budgeting your miracles means that you walk in them until everyone has all they need. Don't hold back, don't save some for later, and don't wait until the end for the bigger miracles. Keep believing and keep them coming until everyone is satisfied.

One of the ways I personally practice this concept is by taking each of my grandkids out for a special day during the summer. It's a day that's just them and me. The day is planned according to their age, and it's called by their first initial. For example,

OVERFLOW

| o • ver • flow |

TO RUN OVER, TO SWELL, RUN OVER THE BRIM OR BANK, TO BE ABUNDANT, ABOUND; EXUBERANT, AS OVERFLOW INTO PLENTY.

Devin gets a "D" day, and everything we do starts with the letter "D." We might start at Hypnotic Donuts, visit a drum store in downtown Denton, and go to a dine-in movie! It's a one-on-one day for spending time together and making memories.

And, here's the best part: There's no budget for the day!

The day is full of unlimited fun, food, movies, games, shopping, and experiences. We take pictures and document the blessings along the way. Each time I do this, it's another learning experience in stretching my faith to give them unlimited blessings.

That's me and my grandkids. Can you only imagine how much more God wants us to stretch our faith for miracles from Him? He wants to show off to us! Our Father God is the ultimate Dad, and He wants to give us not just what we need, but all we want, as well. Contrary to what religion says, it's okay to want things from God! Think about it. God is the One who gave you the desire in the first place.

Why?

So He can be God and fulfill *all* the desires of your heart.

The bottom line is this: God loves you and wants to bless you more than you can handle. Let Him!

It's the beginning of the miracle flow.

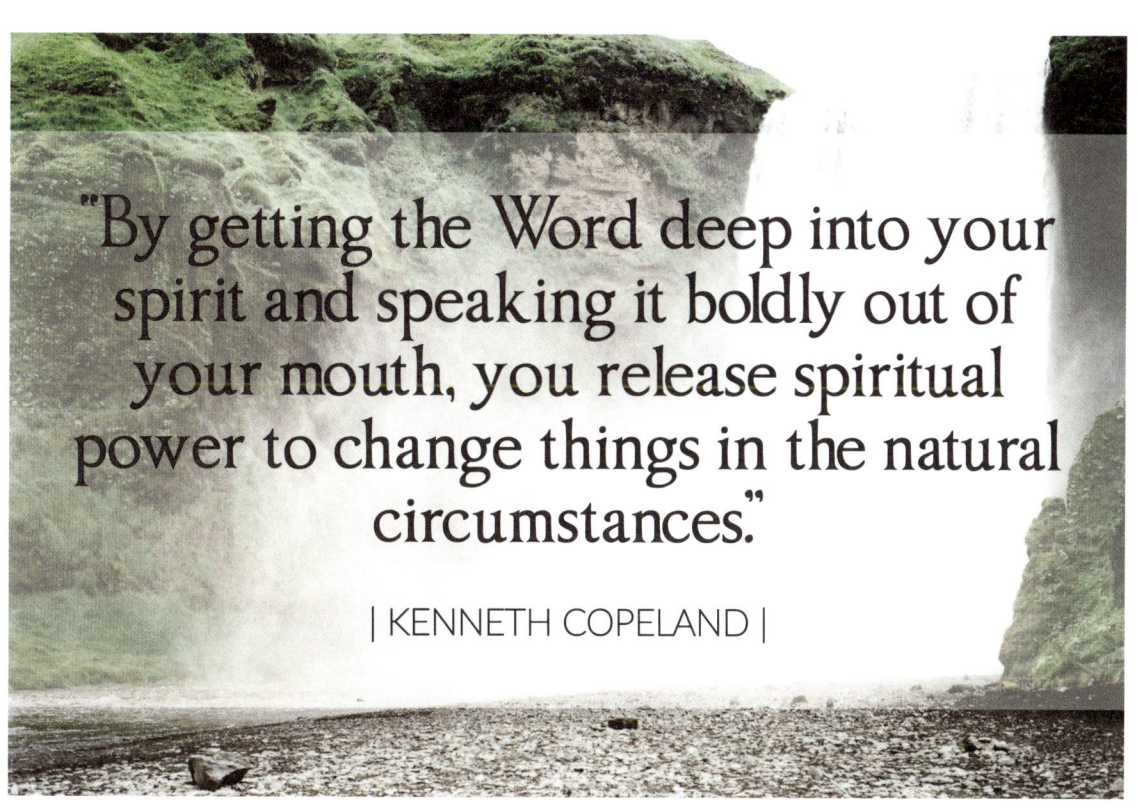

"By getting the Word deep into your spirit and speaking it boldly out of your mouth, you release spiritual power to change things in the natural circumstances."

| KENNETH COPELAND |

Heavenly!

Every Christmas, Cyndy makes these delicious chocolate chip pies for a number of people. It's her way to bless them with love—and, of course, chocolate! One of our friends, who's been in the bakery business for over thirty-five years, describes her pies as "heavenly."

I agree with him!

Now, she doesn't make just one or two pies; it's more like twenty! This way, she can be sure to include everyone on her list, along with others who might pop up. All our friends eagerly await their chocolate chip pie every Christmas. Anything else is a disappointment.

For these gifts, Cyndy spares no expense. Every pie has an abundant supply of chocolate chips—not the cheap ones but the rich, deep, semi-sweet ones. She doesn't use cheap margarine, only genuine butter. Of course, she buys the ingredients all throughout the year, saving them for this special occasion. No wonder our baker friend describes them as "heavenly!"

Isn't that what we desire our lives to be? Heavenly? I know I do. How about you? To have this rich and fulfilling life requires rich ingredients and a belief that God is an unlimited God. It's a choice. You can choose to believe and live this life.

YOU CAN LIVE THE HEAVENLY, FILLIONAIRE LIFE!

Three Things

When the Lord spoke, "Don't budget your miracles," to my heart, three things immediately went off in my spirit.

#1 - PEOPLE BUDGET THEIR MIRACLES

The practice of budgeting God's power is a human reality. People limit God's power all the time. This even happened to Jesus in His home town of Nazareth.

> *"And He could do no mighty work there except that He laid His hands on a few sick people and healed them. And He marveled because of their unbelief. And he went round about the villages, teaching."*
>
> **Mark 6:5-6 (ESV)**

Those closest to Jesus in His home town had a major "choke point." Their experience with Him before His baptism was so normal, that they could not transition into faith and receive any miracles from Him. What was Jesus' response? He taught. What did Jesus teach? That He had come from God, with the anointing of the Spirit, to solve every problem with the power of God. (See Luke 4:18-19.) The same is true today.

The cure for unbelief is hearing the Word.

We need to rid ourselves of any and all hindrances to our faith. God's Word is true. Jesus is anointed by God to do miracles in your life, today. Believe it and then act like it's true.

#2 - PEOPLE LIMIT THEIR MIRACLES

God has an unlimited supply of miraculous power, but it's our choice as to how much we believe and walk in it.

> *"And, behold, there came a leper and worshipped Him, saying 'Lord, if you will, you can make me clean.' And Jesus reached out his hand and touched him saying; 'I will, be cleansed.' And immediately his leprosy was cleansed."*
>
> Matthew 8:2-3 (KJV)

This man knew Jesus had the supernatural ability to remove his disease, as well as every trace of evidence that it had ever existed in his body. He knew it was possible. He even had faith in the power that Jesus exhibited in His ministry, but it wasn't enough.

He knew Jesus *could* but didn't know if He *would*.

This debate still exists in the minds of believers today:

* *"I know Jesus can heal, but does He want to heal me?"*

* *"What is His will?"*

* *"Does He only want to heal me halfway?"*

* *"Maybe Jesus wants to remove the infections but leave the scars?"*

Can you see the limitations that are possible if we reason away His miracle supply? The answer Jesus gave him was: "I WILL!" And He did it—completely, totally, and forever. That's still His answer today.

Don't limit God.

#3 - PEOPLE ARE AFRAID OF "TOO BIG"

God's desire for you is far above what you can think or ever imagine. It's time to release your imagination. When you think as big as you can, when you dream as big as you can, understand that God wants you to have even more! Don't let fear, anxiety, and stress get in your way. Instead, use your faith for love, peace, and overflow. The Bible says it like this:

> *"Now unto Him that is able to do exceeding abundantly above all that we ask or think, according to the power that works in us; to Him be glory in the church by Christ Jesus throughout all ages, world without end. Amen."*
>
> Ephesians 3:20-21 (KJV)

Notice this: There is no budget for "exceeding abundantly above all!" God is able to do miracles far beyond your capacity.

Your limitations in asking can be exceeded.

Your limitations in thinking can be exceeded.

When God does a miracle for His people, He gets the glory.

So, ask yourself, "Why would I want to rob God of getting glory?"

You don't.

So, then why limit yourself to one miracle?

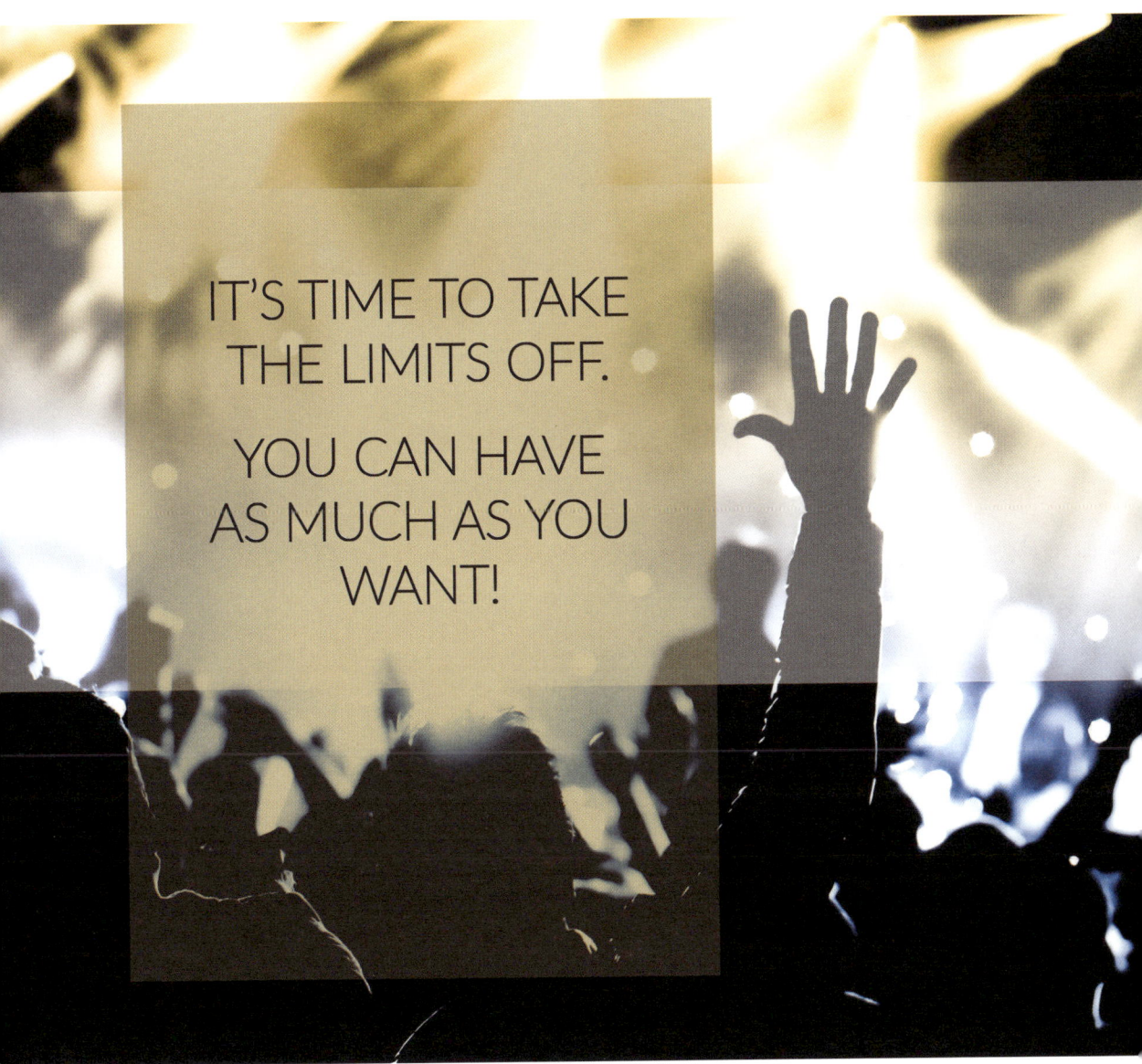

IT'S TIME TO TAKE THE LIMITS OFF.

YOU CAN HAVE AS MUCH AS YOU WANT!

God Loves It

Some of my fondest memories growing up were when my dad and I would leave the house and take a walk together. With five kids in the house, getting time alone with him was very special. Those times together helped shape how I think today.

We would talk about any number of things. I could always tell if my responses were acceptable just by the expressions on his face. If I talked negatively about someone and His response was of disapproval, I quickly re-evaluated my thoughts and made an adjustment. This really helped me to be more open to the opinions of others and become more loving in my approach to people.

Today, I call and talk with my dad on the phone every couple of days. He still has a very strong influence in my life.

In the same way, one of the best things about walking with God is that we have the opportunity to really know

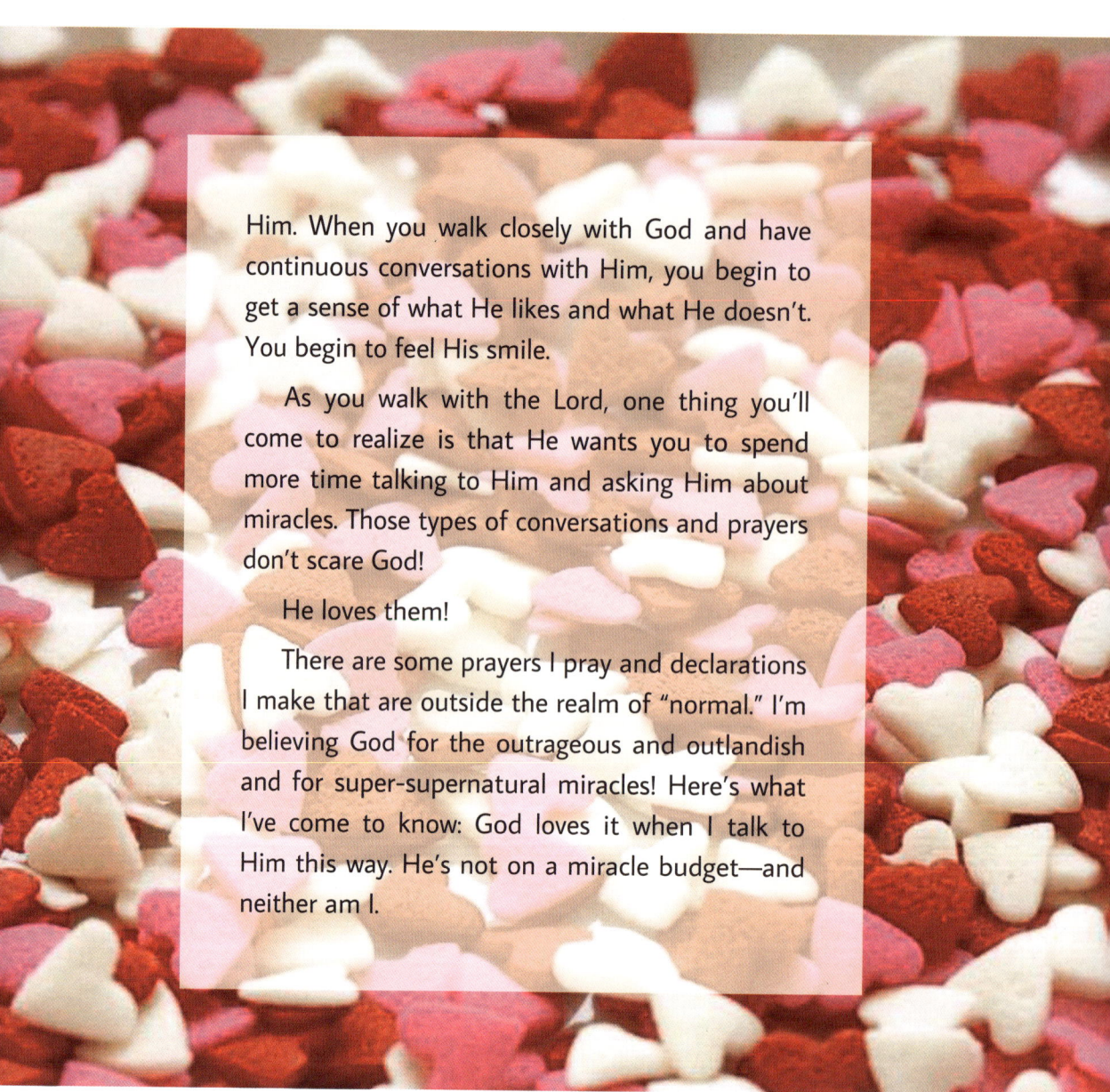

Him. When you walk closely with God and have continuous conversations with Him, you begin to get a sense of what He likes and what He doesn't. You begin to feel His smile.

As you walk with the Lord, one thing you'll come to realize is that He wants you to spend more time talking to Him and asking Him about miracles. Those types of conversations and prayers don't scare God!

He loves them!

There are some prayers I pray and declarations I make that are outside the realm of "normal." I'm believing God for the outrageous and outlandish and for super-supernatural miracles! Here's what I've come to know: God loves it when I talk to Him this way. He's not on a miracle budget—and neither am I.

Two-fold

Times of communion with God are priceless. If you will listen, God will speak. You will learn His voice and get to know His heart. One thing to always remember is, God's Word is His bond. He will never speak something to your heart that contradicts His written Word. If what you feel in your heart doesn't line up with the Word, begin to pray for clearer understanding.

The Word always prevails.

Having the heart of God and knowing the Word of God is a two-fold weapon. Jesus exemplified this when He was tempted by the devil in the wilderness. Not only did He know, "It is written," but He also had the heart of God in the midst of every temptation. Even when the devil tried to use Scripture against Him, Jesus discerned the difference because He knew the Word *and* the Father's heart.

Without a doubt, Pastor Terri Copeland Pearsons demonstrates a life full of the Word and a heart of God better than anyone I've ever seen. She's constantly teaching on prayer and faith; and when she does, it challenges Cyndy and me to listen carefully and grow our faith in every area of life.

To live a FILLIONAIRE life, you need to be challenged to grow regularly! Whenever Cyndy and I are facing a difficult circumstance, we often look at each other and say, "What would Pastor Terri do in this situation?" What a blessing it is to have a friend whose faith lifts you up to greater things, who challenges you to talk with God and believe for more!

The Miracle Zone

FILLIONAIRES practice their faith daily—and it's easier than you may think.

Look at an area of your life that needs improvement. Now, go find scriptures which speak to those areas and read them over and over again. Every time you read them, you're building your faith. Your faith is growing. Your mind is changing. Your limits are being removed.

Every time you build your faith, you prepare for something greater.

For example:

When you believe God for a good parking space at the mall,

You're developing your faith for when you need a first class upgrade on an airplane.

When you believe God for healing of a headache,

You're developing your faith if you need a miracle in your body.

When you believe God for extra birthday money,

You're developing your faith for when you need a new car.

At this moment, Cyndy and I have a particular car that we are using our faith to receive. We're not limiting God. We could go out and purchase it with a loan, but we've decided to use our faith instead. Why? Because we've made the decision to live the FILLIONAIRE life.

We are living in the miracle zone!

God is not on a miracle budget. He's the God of unlimited miracles—and the good news is, He has many miracles available for you. Keep sowing the Word in your spirit. Keep developing your faith. Keep your confession right. Watch what God does on your behalf. When you do your part, God does His part!

FILLIONAIRES are not satisfied with barely getting by or the status quo. We want it all. We want ALL the miracles God has for us! We believe God is an unlimited God.

Fillionaire

STATEGIES

2

. . . FOR <u>NOT</u> BUDGETING YOUR MIRACLES!

* Develop your faith daily for miracles in your life.

* Get faith-filled people around you who believe in miracles.

* Read a scripture out loud ten times daily to build your faith.

* Imagine helping the disciples passing out the bread and fish and then filling up your basket.

* Thank God for miracles in your life today!

DECLARE THESE:

"I develop my faith daily for daily miracles!"

"He rained down manna upon them to eat and gave them food from heaven. Man did eat the bread of angels; He sent them food in abundance." (Psalms 78:24-25, NASB)

"I surround myself with miracle faith people!"

"For you will bless the righteous. LORD, you will surround him with favor as with a shield." (Psalms 5:12, NHEB)

"I work the Word into my life by speaking it ten times in a row!"

"You accepted what we said as the very word of God—which, of course, it is. And this word continues to work in you who believe." (1 Thessalonians 2:13, NLT)

"I imagine myself passing out miracles like the disciples!"

"And Jesus took the loaves; and when he had given thanks, he distributed to the disciples, and the disciples to them that were set down; and likewise of the fishes as much as they would." (John 6:11, KJV)

"I thank God for miracles every day!"

"Even Simon himself believed, and after he was baptized, he stayed close to Philip constantly, and when he saw the signs and great miracles that were occurring, he was amazed." (Acts 8:13, NET)

CHAPTER 3

ALL

| all |

THE ENTIRE THING; THE WHOLE; EVERYTHING DESIRED.

I love Christmas time and everything that goes with it—all the love, giving, family, decorations, music, food (including Cyndy's chocolate chip pies!), and best of all the celebration of Jesus' birthday!

What an awesome reminder of how God loved us so much that He sent His Son to the earth—and He didn't stop halfway. Oh, no. God gave us His ALL!

With eight grandkids, you can only imagine how many presents are stacked deep underneath our tree each year. When those guys hit the door, the first thing on their minds is opening ALL the presents . . . at one time!

Yes, they have their own Christmas trees at home with presents, and they have another set of grandparents with presents for them, too. But that doesn't stop them from wanting to open ALL their presents at our house. In their minds, they know ALL the presents are just for them—and ALL means ALL!

It's the exact same way living the FILLIONAIRE life.

ALL MEANS ALL!

Wrong Thinking

We used to sing a song in church that said, "You are my all in all." It's amazing how we can sing something for so many years yet never live like it's true! But those mindsets are changing. We are becoming FILLIONAIRES, fully aware that our God is an "ALL" God.

Think about these things for a moment:

* How much supply does God have for you?

* How many of your aches and pains does Jesus want to heal?

* How many of your bills does God want to pay?

* How many of your debts does He want to eliminate?

* How many of your needs does the Lord want to meet?

One? A few? Some today and then a few more tomorrow? Maybe, in a couple of years, He might help you see the light at the end of the tunnel? After all, you wouldn't want to be greedy and ask God for too much, right? I mean, He's pretty busy doing bigger things than just helping us insignificant humans, right? There's one word that describes these and other crazy mindsets about God:

WRONG!

That's wrong thinking! It's this kind of thinking that will leave you feeling frustrated and stuck.

A few patterns of wrong thinking that will limit God from fully working in your life are:

"Jesus, I know You can, but I don't know if you will."

Jesus already said, "I will!" (See Matthew 8:3.)

"The Lord giveth, and the Lord taketh away."

No, Satan took away. God was the One giving. (See Job 1:21.)

"Every day I have is one more than I deserve."

"If God didn't spare Jesus, but freely gave Him for our salvation, why wouldn't He also give us all things?" Romans 8:32

"Faith makes all things possible; love makes all things easy."

| Dwight Moody |

I love it when our grandkids ask us for something, and we can give it to them. You might say, "Those kids need to work and earn what they get." Well, there will be plenty of time for that later on in their lives. For now, our job as grandparents is to help them understand the goodness of God on a level that will boost their faith.

Not too long ago, Cyndy and I took our granddaughter, Kendall, for her "K" day. While shopping, she found a cell phone cover she really liked but thought it would be too expensive for us to buy. Before I knew what was happening, Cyndy had walked up to the counter, plopped down the money, and bought it! No questions asked. No fanfare. No begging. She just did it.

Hey, that's what grandparents do, right? Our job is to bless our grandkids.

Later on, at a church bookstore, Kendall saw a girl's Bible she really liked with cute purple and pink flowers on the outside. Again, she didn't ask for it because she thought it cost too much. Once again, it was G-ma to the rescue. BAM! Cyndy just threw down the money and bought it, too.

But this was more than just a purchase; it was an investment. Ever since that day, Cyndy has regularly sent Kendall text messages asking her what great Bible verse she had read that day—out of her purple and pink-flowered Bible. Talk about a God-connection of love! God has used us to help Kendall (and all of our other grandkids) form a mindset about Him that He is an "ALL" God.

They are on their way to living the life of a FILLIONAIRE!

All the Miracles

Maybe you've lived with a limited mindset of God. Maybe the thought of Him being ALL is a bit foreign. That's okay. You can change your thinking. Here are a few verses that will help you gain a clearer understanding of how God desires to meet ALL your needs, problems, and challenges.

"And Jesus went about ALL Galilee, teaching in their synagogues, preaching the gospel of the kingdom, and healing ALL kinds of sickness and ALL kinds of disease among the people. Then His fame went throughout ALL Syria, and they brought to Him ALL sick people who were afflicted with various diseases and torments, and those who were demon possessed, epileptics, and paralytics; and He healed them (ALL)."

Matthew 4:23-24 (NKJV)

"When evening had come, they brought to Him many who were demon-possessed. And He cast out the spirits with a word, and healed ALL who were sick, that it might be fulfilled which was spoken by Isaiah the prophet, saying; 'He Himself took our infirmities and bore our sicknesses.'"

Matthew 8:16-17 (NKJV)

"Then Jesus went about ALL the cities and villages, teaching in their synagogues, preaching the gospel of the kingdom, and healing EVERY sickness and EVERY disease among the people."

Matthew 9:35 (NHEB)

"Then fear came upon EVERY soul, and many wonders and signs were done through the apostles. Now ALL who believed were together, and had ALL things in common, and sold their possessions and goods, and divided them among ALL as anyone had need."

Acts 2:43-45 (NKJV)

You get the point: ALL means ALL—and that's all that all means.

All You Do

Understand, this doesn't mean that all you have to do is sit back and let God heal you if He wants to. Nor does it imply that He will pay your bills if He feels like it. There's another scripture which needs to be included in this section, as well:

"The Lord shall command the blessing upon you in your storehouses, and in ALL that you put your hand to; and he shall bless you in the land which the Lord your God is giving you."

Deuteronomy 28:8 (NKJV)

Did you see the "ALL" God's speaking of? God wants to bless ALL the work of *your* hands. That's right, your "ALL" God wants to bless and prosper ALL *you* do! What that means is, you need to get busy. Give God something He can bless, so you can, in turn, be a blessing.

● ● ● ● ● ● ● ● ● ●

GIVE GOD SOMETHING HE CAN BLESS, SO YOU CAN, IN TURN, BE A BLESSING.

● ● ● ● ● ● ● ● ● ●

A very interesting word in this scripture is the word, "storehouses." We call them warehouses or—better yet—banks, a place where you store your money in a savings account. When you give God something to bless, He promises that ALL you do will multiply. Everything you're believing for will make its way into your hands.

Here's a great thought. When you're blessed, you create things—like jobs and opportunities for others to be blessed. The blessing is not just for you; it's contagious and affects ALL you do, ALL you say, and ALL you are to those around you.

It's time to get busy!

All Grace

Just as there's no budget on God's miracles, He's not stingy with His goodness either. His grace towards you has the ability to bring miracles into your life, and here's the best part:

He's just as willing to bless you as He is able!

"And God is able to make ALL grace (every favor and earthly blessing) come to you in abundance, so that you may always, and under all circumstances, and whatever the need be self-sufficient [possessing enough to require no aid or support and furnished in abundance for every good work and charitable donation.]"

2 Corinthians 9:8 (AMPC)

If you think God's not generous, think again! You're thinking small, believing small, and most likely asking small. FILLIONAIRES don't think that way. We're the ones who believe God and take Him at His Word! We are persuaded that our Heavenly Father has an intense desire to bless us by making all grace abound towards us.

That's why we pray, ask, and expect big things.

We have an "ALL" God.

He makes ALL grace and favor come towards us!

Full Coverage

If you've ever bought insurance—whether it be auto, home, health, etc.— you always look for the most coverage with a reasonable deductible at the price you can afford.

It's common sense.

In the same manner, when you apply for a job, you make sure both the pay and the benefits package will cover your needs and the needs of your family.

In short, you want FULL coverage.

The question now is, why would you demand full coverage in the natural but expect far less from God? It doesn't make much sense does it? The truth is, God has a benefits package, . . . and it's ALL-inclusive!

Just look at the ministry of Jesus. You WON'T find:

* *Nominal* needs met.

* *Halfway* healings.

* *Partial* prosperity.

No! But, what you DO see is the complete expression of what God wants do to in your life—ALL!

* Jesus meets ALL of my needs!

* Jesus heals ALL of my diseases!

* God blesses ALL of the work of my hands!

* He makes ALL grace abound towards me!

* I always have ALL sufficiency in ALL things!

* I always abound!

King David learned firsthand what God's benefits package included. Not only that, he discovered how to keep his coverage current:

"Bless the Lord, oh My soul, and ALL that is within me, bless His holy name! Bless the Lord, O my soul, and forget not ALL His benefits. Who forgives all your iniquities, who heals all your diseases, who redeems your life from destruction, who crowns you with lovingkindness and tender mercies. Who satisfies your mouth with good things, so that your youth is renewed like the eagles."

Psalms 103:1-5 (NKJV)

David knew the proper response to God's benefits package: gratefulness and thankfulness. At every opportunity and in every situation, David gave glory to God for ALL the blessings that came his way—and did they ever come his way!

When David was sent out by his father, Jesse, to bring food to his brothers who were in the army, he saw and heard the biggest man he had ever seen: Goliath. This giant of a man was mocking and challenging the people of God. David's response was classic:

> *"Then David spoke to the men who stood by Him, saying: What shall be done for the man who kills this Philistine and takes away the reproach from Israel? For who is this uncircumcised Philistine, that He should defy the armies of the Living God?"*
>
> 1 Samuel 17:26 (KJV)

In other words, "Who do you think you are and how dare you talk to us that way?"

The soldiers then explained to David the benefits package King Saul was offering to the one who slayed the giant. It included great riches, King Saul's daughter in marriage, and tax exemption for life. Those sounded good to David, so he accepted the challenge.

It's interesting how David never asked for a written contract or any guarantees. He didn't have to fast and pray or take days to ponder the offer. He had been training for this moment his entire life. David simply believed and acted as if God was with Him.

All he needed was a sling, some stones, and his faith in God. The giant was laughing, but David got the last laugh. In the end, Goliath was defeated, God got the glory, and David got the girl!

When you follow his life and story, David's full coverage benefits plan included:

* Deliverance from lions, giants, and bears . . . oh, my!

* First in line to become king.

* Marrying the king's daughter.

* ALL the spoils ALL the time.

* Theft recovery.

* Forgiveness of sin.

* Youth renewal.

* Lawsuit protection. (to cover him while dancing in his underwear in public!)

David was benefits-minded. He *knew* his full-coverage-providing, "ALL" God! In short, David was a FILLIONAIRE.

Let's live *that* kind of life—the kind that knows our Creator is not only willing to miraculously take care of us but also longs for us to ask Him for miracles every day.

The FILLIONAIRE life—that's YOUR life!

GOD is able to bestow EVERY blessing ON YOU IN abundance, so that richly enjoying **ALL** sufficiency at **ALL** times, you may have ample means for **ALL** good works.

2 Corinthians 9:8

| Weymouth New Testament |

Fillionaire
STRATEGIES
#3

. . . FOR "ALL"

* Believe in God's willingness; He said, "I will."
* Be bold in prayer; He will do it all!
* Put your hands on it; He will bless it all!
* Sign up for His program; remember ALL His benefits!

DECLARE THESE:

"I believe in God's willingness because He already said, 'I will!'"

"This is the covenant that I will make with them after those days, saith the Lord, I will put my laws into their hearts, and in their minds will I write them;" (Hebrews 10:16, WEB)

"I am bold in my prayers because God will do it all!"

"The righteous are bold as a young lion." (Proverbs 28:1b, JUB)

"I put my hands on what I need because God will bless it all!"

"For the LORD your God will bless you in all your harvest and in all the work of your hands, and your joy will be complete." (Deuteronomy 16:15, NIV)

"I sign up for God's benefits program because He covers it all!"

"This God—his way is perfect; the word of the LORD proves true; he is a shield for all those who take refuge in him." (2 Samuel 22:31, ESV)

"I remember all His benefits and give God all the glory!"

"And I saw the glory of the God of Israel coming from the east. His voice was like the roar of rushing waters, and the land was radiant with his glory." (Ezekiel 43:2, NIV)

CHAPTER 4

Filled with All
the Fullness

When our daughter-in-law, Amy, had her first baby (and our first grand-baby), she loved that child with everything inside her. Being a first-time mom, her entire focus was to love, nurture, and provide for that boy in every way she could—and she did an awesome job.

But then, something happened.

She became pregnant with child number two!

Joy and elation was also met with some concern about this baby. Thoughts ran through her mind like:

* My heart is already full of love.

* Where will more love come from?

* Do I have the capacity to love more?

The day came, and she gave birth to baby number two. And guess what? Her heart was flooded with as much love for baby number two as baby number one. God filled her heart to overflowing for both. Now, Jesse and Amy have four children who they love with all their hearts.

The love of a mom has no limits. The same is true concerning God's love towards you. His love knows no limits! He doesn't live in the realm of limitation. His love is endless. His love is boundless.

One of the best explanations of this love is found in Ephesians Chapter 3. Here, the apostle Paul uses a beautiful continuous thread of words to describe eternal things which surpass our human knowledge. Then he prays for us, that we would be strengthened with all might to grasp what he is saying.

After expounding on the vastness of God, Paul then turns his attention to the love of God:

> *"So that Christ may dwell in your hearts through faith. And I pray that you, being rooted and grounded in love, may have power, together with all the saints, to comprehend the length and width and height and depth of His love."*

Ephesians 3:17-18 (BSB)

Paul uses four terms to try and help us measure the truly unmeasurable:

Length

How long is the love of Christ? Too long. Longer than eternity.

Width

How wide is the love of Christ? Too wide. Wider than forever.

Height

How high is the love of Christ? Too high. Higher than the heavens.

Depth

How deep is the love of Christ? Deeper than hell, which He proved by going there and defeating the devil.

You can never exhaust the love of God! His desire is for us to know—personally and experientially—how massive His love is for us, His children. When we come to this realization, then we are well on our way to fullness—FULLNESS in Him!

FILLED

| filled |

THE STATE OF ABOUNDING OR BEING IN GREAT PLENTY, ABUNDANCE, WEALTH, AFFLUENCE, TO LEAVE NO PART VACANT.

Filled with His Fullness

Look at how Paul finishes this passage:

"and to know this love that surpasses knowledge—that you may be filled to the measure of all the fullness of God."

Ephesians 3:19 (NIV)

Wow! When the reality of His love comes in, you live the FILLIONAIRE life—FILLED with the FULLNESS of God. I like that—FILLED with ALL His fullness.

Not just selected areas of your life—in every area!

So, now the question is: What are you full of?

If we are constantly consumed with our wants, needs, thoughts, and ways, etc., then we cannot be filled with His fullness. Anything other than His love in us means we are not filled with Him. If we carry resentment, fear, bitterness, hatred, jealousy, envy, division, strife, or hurt in our hearts, then we're not allowing His love to free us, cleanse us, and fill us with all His goodness.

His fullness becomes evident in our lives when we change our focus and become consumed with the revelation of His all-fulfilling love. His love is bigger, wider, longer, and deeper than anything in the universe. When we're good, when we're bad, when we're right, when we're wrong—it doesn't change the fact that God's love is unconditional.

God's love is as big as God Himself. If we're filled with His love, then we're filled with God—and that makes us FILLIONAIRES!

"and [that you may come] to know [practically, through personal experience] the love of Christ which far surpasses [mere] knowledge [without experience], that you may be FILLED up [throughout your being] to ALL the FULLNESS of God [so that you may have the richest experience of God's presence in your lives, completely FILLED and flooded with God Himself]."

Ephesians 3:19
| Amplified Bible Classic Edition |

The Overflow

When you're filled with His fullness, God's love, power, and ability flow out of you to meet the needs of others and to heal broken lives. It's very simple: A FILLIONAIRE lives out of His overflow.

When God is fulfilling all your needs, you have plenty left over to help others with their needs. When you're so full of blessings, healing, strength, and joy that it flows out of you, everyone around you will be completely blessed, as well.

FILLIONAIRES are like water; they flow downhill and fill up every available space with their substance. The fluid nature of water combined with the force of gravity results in the filling effect.

A few years ago, Cyndy and I went to Toronto, Canada to attend a wedding for our good friend, Pastor Anthony Does, whom we have known and have been a part of his life for many years now. He was marrying a beautiful girl, Sonja, and we didn't want to miss the chance to meet her and celebrate their lives together.

While we were there, we took in a visit to Niagara Falls from the Canadian side. It's amazing how different the view is from that side, versus the U.S. side of the river.

Niagara Falls is actually composed of three different waterfalls, which form the highest flow rate of any other waterfall in the world and has a vertical drop of more than one hundred and sixty-five feet. The roaring waters create so much energy that the flow is utilized to create hydroelectric power. There's only one word to describe it:

Awesome!

Watching the water crash over the falls is like seeing a demonstration of God's vast fullness right before your very eyes. It reminded me of the scripture:

"FOR THE EARTH SHALL BE FILLED WITH THE KNOWLEDGE OF THE GLORY OF THE LORD, AS THE WATERS COVER THE SEA."

HABAKKUK 2:14
| King James Version |

Have you ever thought, "How full is the sea?"

The answer is easy. However much water there is, that's how much of the sea is covered.

Think of it this way. If someone tried to make a hole in the ocean by removing water out from the middle of it, it wouldn't work, would it? In the same way, you cannot exhaust the miracle power of God. If you tried to make a void in the middle of it, God would fill it back up immediately with His love and grace.

His love and grace are an ever-flowing current, rushing to fulfill every need.

The Bible confirms it.

"And of His FULLNESS have we ALL received and grace for grace."

John 1:16 (KJV)

"For it pleased the Father that in Him should ALL FULLNESS dwell."

Colossians 1:19 (KJV)

"For in Him dwells ALL the FULLNESS of the Godhead bodily;"

Colossians 2:9 (NKJV)

"God cannot use you as
He wishes until you come in
the fullness of His glory."

| George Washington Carver |

Dwelling in His Fullness

Your dwelling is where you live, where you experience life with those you love, and where you call home. It's also a reflection of you. Your favorite colors, designs, textures, and décor are all represented in your dwelling.

Everywhere you look, it's you!

If you're married, you probably chose a home that was comfortable and cozy for you and your spouse. Then, you worked together and FILLED it up with furniture and decorations that represented your lives together. That was a good start . . . until children came along!

Now, you need a larger house . . . that can be FILLED with more stuff.

So, you move into a larger house to accommodate your growing family. It's not long before it's full. But wait! Kids don't stay toddlers forever; they grow up, and you discover that your taste in decorating has probably changed, as well. So, baby beds and old decorations find a new home in the garage, while bigger stuff takes their place in your house . . . and then . . . before long, . . .

. . . the garage is FILLED.

Eventually, the garage starts to overflow. Then you start giving things away as a blessing to others.

Your dwelling is always in a continual state of filling up to its fullness—but that's not the only thing. Just as you fill your empty house with furniture and heart-warming decorations, your heart also longs to be full with love and companionship.

If you're single, you rely mostly on your family and friendships to fill your time, attention, and need for connection.

If you're married, your primary source of fulfillment comes from your spouse and children. But, let me insert something here. Too many married couples just exist together. They live in the same house, eat at the same dinner table, raise the same kids, sleep in the same bed, but have practically no emotional, spiritual, or physical connection whatsoever.

One of the things Cyndy and I have asked pastors for years is: "If you took the ministry, your church, your kids, and your relatives out of your life, what would your marriage look like?"

This question really is for anyone who's married or is thinking about marriage. There's hardly any greater loneliness than being lonely while surrounded by your spouse and children.

Marriages must be constantly filled with the goodness of God. It's His will to fill your marriage, but you must *purposely decide* to keep it full.

Special occasions—like wedding anniversaries—are a perfect time to work on your closeness, but you have to make a determined effort to keep it filled with your love for each other.

Cyndy and I just celebrated our fortieth anniversary—and we did it right! We spent the week at an all-inclusive resort on a gorgeous beach. Before we left our house, we made the commitment to each other: NO WORK! We walked on the beach, drank coffee while watching the sunrise, slept late, worked on our tans, and enjoyed fabulous meals together. At the end of our celebration week, we were FILLED.

FILLED with love for one another.

FILLED with vision for our future.

We were dwelling in the FULLNESS of God.

The Vacuum Effect

Whatever is lacking in your life creates a space that's longing to be filled. I call it "The Vacuum Effect." Empty relationships long to be filled. Hollow emotions cry out to be filled. Lonely marriages need filling. Even your spirit man, when empty, must be filled with the presence of God.

You wouldn't live in an empty house and sleep on the floor if you didn't have to, would you? Of course not.

Just like you fill your house with furniture and decorations and fill your life with family and friends, your spiritual life needs filling, as well. Going long periods of time without spending time talking to God or feeding on His Word will leave you spiritually dry and empty.

This is why it's vitally important to belong to a good church with a faith-filled pastor. It will keep you connected to the family of God and keep your spirit filled.

Living the FILLIONAIRE life is living a life FULL of God, where He invades and fills every part of your life: your marriage, your emotions, your finances, dreams, your spirit man, your future, your relationships with family and friends, your social life, your health, your mind, and your thoughts—every part!

Are you allowing God to fill your life, or are you consumed with your own self? Are you filled with His fullness? Are you so filled that you live out of the overflow? Are you dwelling in His fullness, day-in and day-out? If you are, then . . .

WELCOME TO THE FILLIONAIRE LIFE!

Fillionaire
STRATEGIES #4

. . . FOR FULLNESS!

* Determine to grasp God's greatness! He is bigger than anything.

* Start by receiving His big love. Stretch your heart every day.

* Focus on the vastness of His grace, not on the limits of this life.

* Let His fullness flow! Free yourself of hindering thoughts.

* Live in His fullness! Dream your way into your future.

DECLARE THESE:

"I determine to grasp God's greatness, because He's bigger than any-thing!"

"How precious to me are your thoughts, God! How vast is the sum of them!" (Psalms 139:17, NIV)

"I receive His big love by strengthening my heart every day!"

"The LORD is my strength and shield. I trust him with all my heart. He helps me, and my heart is filled with joy. I burst out in songs of thanksgiving." (Psalms 28:7, NLB)

"I focus on the vastness of His grace, not on life's limitations!"

"To focus our minds on the human nature leads to death, but to focus our minds on the Spirit leads to life and peace." (Romans 8:6, ISV)

"I let the fullness of God flow in my thought life!"

"I have thought about my life, and I have directed my feet back to your written instructions." (Psalms 119:59, GW)

"I live in the fullness of God and dream my way into my future!"

"I know the plans that I have for you, declares the LORD. They are plans for peace and not disaster, plans to give you a future filled with hope." (Jeremiah 29:11, GW)

Take the Limitations Off

CHAPTER 5

ere we go again! Another Sunday morning while on our way to church, I distinctly heard these words in my spirit: "Take the limitations off of Me because I have taken the limitations off of you!"

I actually didn't realize that I had been limiting God or that I even had a limitation mindset, but I certainly wanted to align myself to His plans and not hinder the miracles of God in my life! So, I started doing what comes natural for me when I hear the Lord speak:

I began meditating on what I heard.

God is moving in such a way that the Body of Christ can rise above every natural obstacle and live a FILLIONAIRE life! The future is bright and limitations have to go. What kind of limitations am I talking about?

Here are a few:

No Financial Limitations

Prosperity belongs to us. The amount of money that is in the world today is nothing short of astounding. Just the highway improvements alone, where we live, are projected to cost over four billion dollars this year. There's no shortage of money, but here's the best news:

THERE'S NO SHORTAGE ON GOD'S ABILITY EITHER.

With God's ability to turn nations, influence hearts, and change circumstances, you have access to all the resources on the planet! It's time to take a step beyond what you have already experienced. Step into the miracle realm. You have a God who's willing to supernaturally create whatever you need—even if it doesn't exist!

Think about the Children of Israel in the Old Testament. When they were in the desert with no food source available, God made food appear on the ground every morning. He even told them how much to gather. They couldn't even save any for the next day because it would go bad. This manna only had a one-day shelf life! Each day was another lesson in trusting God.

UNLIMITED

| un • lim • it • ed |

HAVING NO BOUNDS, UNCONFINED, NOT RESTRAINED.

Every day, God showed up and made food out of nothing.

In the New Testament, Jesus taught us to consider the birds of the air. They don't sow or reap, and yet God feeds them every day. So, what do you have to worry about? What Jesus was saying was, "Don't limit God to whatever resources you have stored away. Trust Him to provide what you need for today."

Miracles are all around you right now.

Jesus also said that all things are possible to him who believes. (See Mark 9:23.) Believes what? Whatever! If you need a thousand dollars, believe He will supply it. What if you need ten thousand dollars? All things are possible. Don't limit Him to your natural resources or any amounts; He said ALL THINGS!

Whether it's thousands, millions, billions, or more, believe that He is able to supply it. Whatever you need to accomplish the things He's asking you to do, He will provide, so that you can confidently go forward.

"When your spirit, by the Holy Spirit, prays, it is prayer as deep and wide as the Spirit of God Himself. It surpasses time, distance, and all natural borders. It knows no limitations."

| Pastor Terri Copeland Pearsons |

No Health Limitations

Healing belongs to us. When Jesus gave His disciples power over all sickness, disease, and evil spirits of infirmity, they were surprised at how easy it was to use it. After seeing the healing power of God manifested, they returned with joy, excited that it worked.

And it worked every time!

Practically no one stirs my faith for more of God than Smith Wigglesworth. I love reading his books, and I've even visited his hometown in Bradford, England. One of his stories has stuck in my mind for years.

One day while Smith Wigglesworth was praying for a woman in the hospital, she died. But that didn't stop this mighty man of God. He lifted her out of bed, stood her against the wall, and shouted, "In the name of Jesus, I rebuke this death!" Immediately, her whole body began to shake. Then he said, "In the name of Jesus, walk!"—and that's exactly what she did!

Healing is easy; unbelief is a struggle. Sometimes, people's heads can short-circuit their faith. It doesn't matter what caused your condition, even if you *think* you "deserved" it by doing something harmful to your body. It doesn't matter how long it's been there. God's healing power is available to you, twenty-four-seven—and just like salvation, it's yours to receive by faith. Jesus' sacrifice

● ● ● ● ● ● ● ● ● ● ● ● ● ● ●

IT'S JUST AS MUCH GOD'S WILL TO HEAL YOU
AS IT WAS TO SAVE YOU.

● ● ● ● ● ● ● ● ● ● ● ● ● ● ●

paid for both your salvation *and* your healing at the same time. It's just as much God's will to heal you as it was to save you.

It goes even further than that. What God does *for* you, He wants to do *through* you.

Your healing isn't just for you. God wants your testimony of His miracle-working power to encourage others, so that they suddenly have faith to be healed, too!

* * * * * * * * * * * * * * *

DON'T LIMIT GOD IN YOUR BODY. HE WANTS TO HEAL, STRENGTHEN, AND EMPOWER YOU TO DO EVERYTHING HE'S CALLED YOU TO DO.

* * * * * * * * * * * * * * *

Don't limit God in your body. He wants to heal, strengthen, and empower you to do everything He's called you to do. Get rid of all your excuses. Be healed, so you can do the will of God for your life. He's not holding anything back. God gave His best—His Son, Jesus—so that you could walk in His grace, glory, and power! (See Romans 8:32.)

You are not limited by sickness! Tell your body to line up with God's plans, and be healed. It's not hard or difficult. Choose to believe and stop doubting.

Take the limits off of God's healing power.

No Age Limitations

What would you think if someone seventy-five years old wanted to start a church? All the church planting organizations would call that person senile or flat-out crazy! But, what would God say? Abraham was seventy-five when he started, and he lived one hundred more years walking by faith like it was no big deal.

Do you think eighty years of age is too old to make a difference in this world? God didn't. Moses was eighty when God anointed him to lead the Children of Israel out of Egypt—and then he led them for forty more years.

Kenneth Copeland turned eighty years old this year, and there's not a "slow down" gear found in him. Retirement isn't even in his vocabulary. As a matter of fact, he's traveling the world and preaching with a renewed strength and purpose. Twice recently, Cyndy and I sat in meetings where he preached and recorded five television broadcasts all in one night . . . for three nights in a row! It was awesome!

When I grow up, I want to be just like him.

"With long life will I satisfy him . . ."
Psalms 91:16a (NKJV)

There are no age limitations with God—on both ends of the spectrum. You can never be too old or too young.

* David was about fifteen years old when he killed Goliath.

* Mary was close to fourteen when she gave birth to Jesus.

* Jeremiah was just a teenager when God called him to shake the nations. God even told him to never say he was too young! (See Jeremiah 1:7.)

* As teenagers in a foreign land, Daniel, Shadrach, Meshach, and Abednego all stood tall for God.

* A little boy's "Happy Meal™" fed over twenty thousand people when Jesus multiplied it.

Young or old, God can use anyone at any age for anything He wants. In the end, He gets all the glory because without Him, we can do nothing. So, what difference does age make anyway? Just think about how old God is!

And He can do anything!

"Great is our Lord and of great power; his understanding is inexhaustible and boundless."

Psalms 147:5

| Amplified Bible Classic Edition |

No Time Limitations

Have you ever wished there were more hours in a day? Have you ever run out of time, and it caused untold amounts of stress in your life? How many times have you ever felt the pressure to buy something quickly because the eBay auction was almost over or the clock was running down on the Home Shopping Network? It's easy to see that time can be a very limiting factor.

It's amazing that Jesus never seemed to be in a hurry. Why? Because He was always in the right place at the right time, doing the right thing. When He heard that His friend Lazarus was about to die, Jesus wasn't moved by other people's urgency. Time did not limit nor dictate His actions. He stayed put for a few more days and then, at the right time, made His way to Lazarus—who had died three days prior.

When He arrived, people were an emotional mess! Mary and Martha, Lazarus' sisters, were highly upset that Jesus didn't respond quicker. Everyone was weeping, judging, questioning, and grieving—everyone except Jesus, that is.

Jesus operated on a totally different time clock: Eternal Standard Time. It didn't matter how many days had gone by or how long Lazarus was dead, the final outcome would've been the same—and God would still have gotten the glory.

Without any urgency, Jesus made His way to the tomb and then did what He always did: obeyed the Father. He told them to roll away the stone and then called Lazarus out of death and into life. In an instant, grief turned into amazement. Tears of joy replaced sobs of sadness. Judging and questioning changed to shouts of rejoicing and praise.

God is not limited by time, and neither are we.

Matthew 27:52 also proves that we're not limited by time. When Jesus was crucified, many Old Testament saints came out of their graves and started preaching in Jerusalem! Obviously, there was no expiration date on their ministries, even though they had been dead for hundreds of years.

Talk about stretching your faith for miracles!

Don't be limited by time. Don't be in a hurry.

WALK WITH GOD, AND WATCH HIS
GLORY MOVE YOU INTO A REALM THAT IS
UNAFFECTED BY THE CLOCK. ETERNITY
IS NOT LIMITED!

No Space Limitations

Wouldn't it be cool to be in two places at once? Or just imagine being instantly translated to somewhere else in a moment of time. It might not be as far-fetched as you imagine.

Think with me for a moment.

The Bible says that God is light. Light travels at the speed of roughly 186,000 miles per second. So, what if we learned to walk with Him in such a way that we could instantly appear in a room? That's what Jesus did after He was raised from the dead. Then, when He was done talking to His friends, He disappeared. Could it be that He simply slowed down from light speed for a bit to visit with the apostles and then shifted back and disappeared? Whatever the case, the truth remains:

SPACE IS NOT A LIMITING FACTOR IN THE ETERNITY ZONE!

I pray that from his glorious, unlimited resources he will empower you with inner strength through his Spirit.

Ephesians 3:16
| New Living Translation |

We know that there's no distance in prayer, right? That we can pray for someone on the other side of the planet or even astronauts in outer space and God will answer that prayer—that's prayer traveling at Godspeed. So, since God is everywhere all at once, what's stopping Him from instantly moving you from one place to another? If you need to be there, God will get you there!

H. B. Garlock, a missionary to Africa, relayed a story like this in his book, *Before We Kill and Eat You*. He tells of a time when he received news that a friend of his was sick. Under normal circumstances, travel to that village would take several days. Nevertheless, he began his long journey to go pray for his friend's healing.

When Brother Garlock came upon a certain river, he was unable to cross it due to the heavy rains produced from the monsoon season. Normally, he would have crossed with a small boat, but the once calm river was now a raging force of water more than a mile wide. Desperate to see his friend, Brother Garlock closed his eyes and prayed. God gave him peace in his heart about the whole situation, so he said, "Amen." Then he opened his eyes and suddenly realized something had changed.

He was standing on the other side of that river!

H. B. Garlock's son, John, who was one of my instructors in college, retold this story one day to our class. I will forever remember him telling it. It definitely had the "WOW!" effect on me. It made me believe that there are no space limitations with God!

● ● ● ● ● ● ● ● ● ● ● ● ● ●

No "Fear of Man" Limitations

During the time Jesus walked on the earth, the Jewish people suffered terrible bondage to the Romans— so much so, that they were afraid for their well-being. Saying or doing the wrong thing could lead to imprisonment or the loss of everything they owned.

They were also in bondage to their religious leaders. Breaking the Jewish laws meant possible death by stoning. All of their bondages and fears shared a common denominator: the fear of man.

No wonder Jesus was so popular! He gave no thought to the opinion of others because He always acted in direct obedience to the Father. As a result, He updated the law for the Jews in the spirit of love, which surprised everybody. Jesus was not limited by the fear of man, thus His faith in God was unlimited.

Perfect love operates above the fear of man realm.

Take Them Off

FILLIONAIRES realize that the only thing limiting God is us! What are we willing to believe Him for? Think, for a moment, about Joshua. He commanded the sun to stand still, so he could defeat the enemy army; and God didn't argue. He just did it. Imagine what we could do . . . if we simply believed that *all things* are possible with our God! The sky is not the limit.

THERE ARE NO LIMITS!

One Sunday morning while at our home church, Eagle Mountain International Church, the Lord gave me a prophetic word along these lines:

"'No more limitations. I am taking them off. The things that have held you back in the past—they are not going to hold you back in the future. I have taken them off.'

'If I can walk on water, then you can walk on water. If I can be in one place in a moment of time and in another place at the next moment, then you can be in one place and then in the next moment at another place.'"

"God says, 'I have taken off the limitations.' So, God says, 'Believe bigger, act bigger, speak bigger, move bigger, expect bigger, think bigger, and go forward, knowing that I am in your future.'

'I have crafted every single step; I have crafted every single word in your heart. Begin to release it on your circumstances, begin to release it on your future, begin to release it on your destiny.'

'Your destiny is much bigger than you have been thinking, so think bigger. Your destiny is much bigger than you have been asking, so ask bigger.' God says, 'Take the limitations off of Me because I have taken the limitations off of you!'"

FILLIONAIRES LEARN TO THINK, BELIEVE, ASK, ACT, SPEAK, MOVE, AND LIVE WITH NO LIMITS.

Fillionaire
STRATEGIES
#5

... FOR AN UNLIMITED LIFESTYLE

* Take the limitations off of God.
* Believe for God-sized provisions.
* Believe for heavenly health.
* Believe for youth renewal.
* Believe for miracles in time.
* Believe for travel miracles.
* Believe that your faith is strong enough to accomplish anything!

DECLARE THESE:

"I take the limitations off of God!"

"Even perfection has its limits, but your commands have no limit." (Psalms 119:96, NLT)

"I believe for God-sized provisions!"

"I will provide the priests with abundant provisions. My people will be filled to the full with the good things I provide." (Jeremiah 31:14, NET)

"I believe God for healing, health and renewal in my body!"

"Behold, I will bring to it health and healing, and I will heal them and reveal to them abundance of prosperity and security." (Jeremiah 33:6, ESV)

"I move past time and space limitations and live in the spirit!"

"For He whom God has sent speaks God's words; for God does not give the Spirit with limitations." (John 3:34, WNT)

"My faith for miracles is working!"

"I persevered in demonstrating among you the marks of a true apostle, including signs, wonders and miracles." (2 Corinthians 12:12, NIV)

CHAPTER 6

REVEALED

| re • vealed |

DISCOVERED, MADE KNOWN.

It never ceases to amaze me how someone can read a scripture for years, and then one day, hear the exact same passage and BAM! All the lights come on, and it explodes in your spirit.

Such was my experience one Sunday morning. I have no idea how many times I've read Exodus 34:10 over the years. But that morning when Pastor George Pearsons read it, it was a game changer.

"And He said, 'Behold, I make a covenant. Before all your people I will do marvels such as have not been done in all the earth, nor in any nation, and all the people among whom you are shall see the work of the Lord. For it is an awesome thing that I will do with you.'"

(NKJV)

God is going to do things for us that have never been seen before.

As soon as Pastor Pearsons finished reading, I began thinking of the things that have already been seen. Three categories came to mind:

1. Things you have seen and experienced personally.

2. Things others have seen and have shared their experiences with you.

3. Things that people in history experienced and documented.

Then I thought, "What has *never* been seen before?" I knew to go to *this* place would take some creative imagination, especially since no one had ever seen them. At that moment, the Lord brought something to my remembrance—something I had seen in my spirit several years ago that has yet to be manifested in the natural.

Some years ago, Cyndy and I had the awesome privilege of conducting youth meetings for Kenneth Copeland's Believers' Conventions. During one of those meetings, I saw something amazing. It really was an open vision. The picture was very clear, but it was like watching a movie.

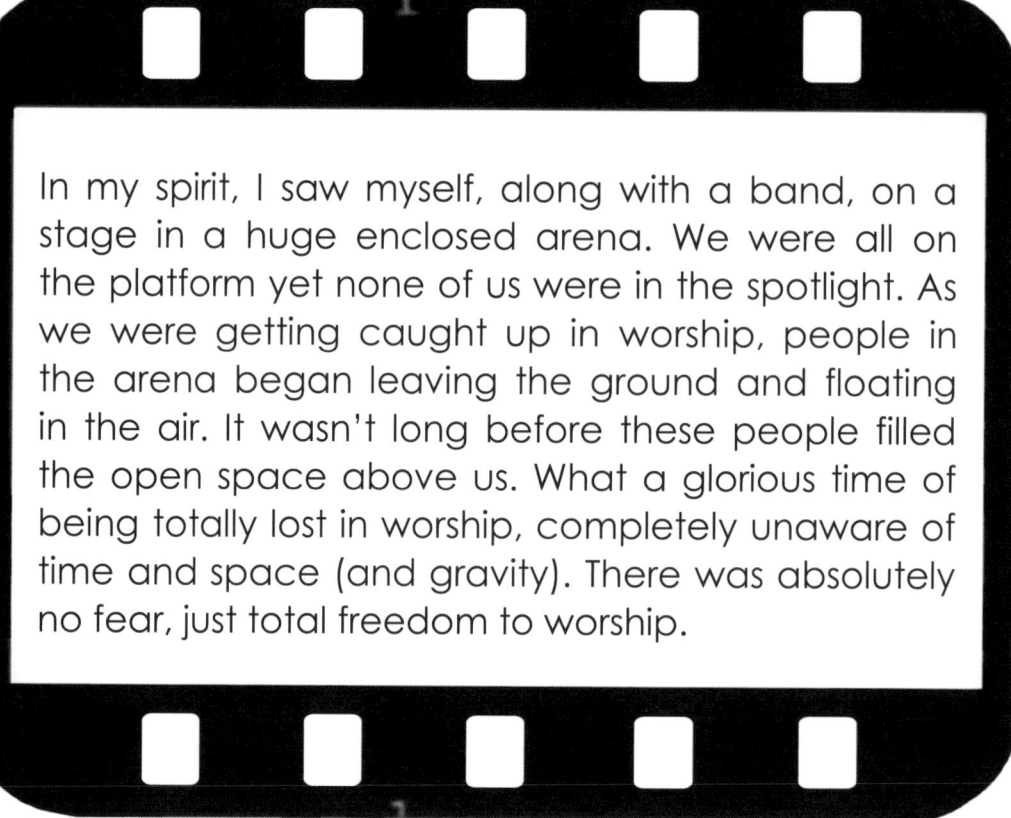

In my spirit, I saw myself, along with a band, on a stage in a huge enclosed arena. We were all on the platform yet none of us were in the spotlight. As we were getting caught up in worship, people in the arena began leaving the ground and floating in the air. It wasn't long before these people filled the open space above us. What a glorious time of being totally lost in worship, completely unaware of time and space (and gravity). There was absolutely no fear, just total freedom to worship.

Recalling that vision fired up my imagination, to say the least! Now it was time to stretch my faith and think of other things never seen before.

Here are few things the Holy Ghost brought to my spirit:

Large Group Translations

FILLIONAIRE, dream with me for a moment. What if entire churches were divinely translated to other nations for evangelism? The Bible talks about such a thing:

* **Single Person Translation:.** Acts Chapter 8 tells the story of Philip, a man who was translated to another city after baptizing the Ethiopian Eunuch.

* **Small Group Translation:** In John Chapter 6, the disciples were threatened by a huge storm while in the middle of a lake. Out of nowhere, Jesus came walking on the water and said, "Do not be afraid." The moment He stepped into the boat, they were all translated to the shore.

Think about this: If Jesus can transport Himself, the whole boat, and all twelve disciples halfway across the Sea of Galilee in a moment, why not an entire congregation today?

He can—and He will! Boldly confess with me:

"THIS WILL HAPPEN TO ME!"

Supernatural Glory Tent

Think about this one for a minute. What if multiplied thousands of people showed up at church unexpectedly, so God created a spiritual tabernacle that covered everyone with the shade of His glory? What if He also provided an invisible glory floor, so that when people were overwhelmed by His presence and fell down, they floated just above the ground? Sounds pretty amazing!

If this scene is stretching your imagination and your faith (which I hope it is!), think about how God covered the Children of Israel with a cloud of glory in the wilderness.

The Bible says, He's the same yesterday, today, and forever. If God did that for His people under the Old Covenant, then why can't He create a supernatural tabernacle today for the multitudes who are coming into the Kingdom?

I believe He can—and He will!

Boldly confess this with me:

"I MAY HAVE NEVER SEEN THE GLORY OF THE LORD LIKE THIS BEFORE, BUT I WILL!"

Special Delivery Finances

One of the seven names for God is Jehovah Jireh, "the Lord our Provider," but far too many Christians today never experience God in that way. To them, He's the God who withholds.

That's not how FILLIONAIRES think!

The Bible says the earth is the Lord's and everything in it. (See Psalms 24:1.) Since He owns it all anyway, don't you think He can load you up with super-natural finances in whatever way He chooses?

He's willing, but you must believe!

Stretch your imagination again with me. What if duffle bags full of cash from drug deals or other worldly business deals supernaturally appeared on the front doors of churches and ministries, all disguised as anonymous donations? God's provision can come from anywhere!

One time, Jesus and Peter needed money to pay their taxes. (All the other disciples were too young to pay taxes.) Jesus' method of finding the money was a bit unconventional. He told Peter to throw a small hook into a big lake. When he did, the first fish he caught had enough money in its mouth to pay the entire tax bill!

Who ever heard of fish swimming around with valuable coins in their mouths? And yet, it happened.

In the same way, God can send angels to take the wealth of the wicked and bring it right to your front door!

Can you believe? If so, confess this with me:

"I'M LOOKING FOR BAGS OF MONEY TO SHOW UP
ANYTIME, ANYWHERE, UNEXPECTEDLY!"

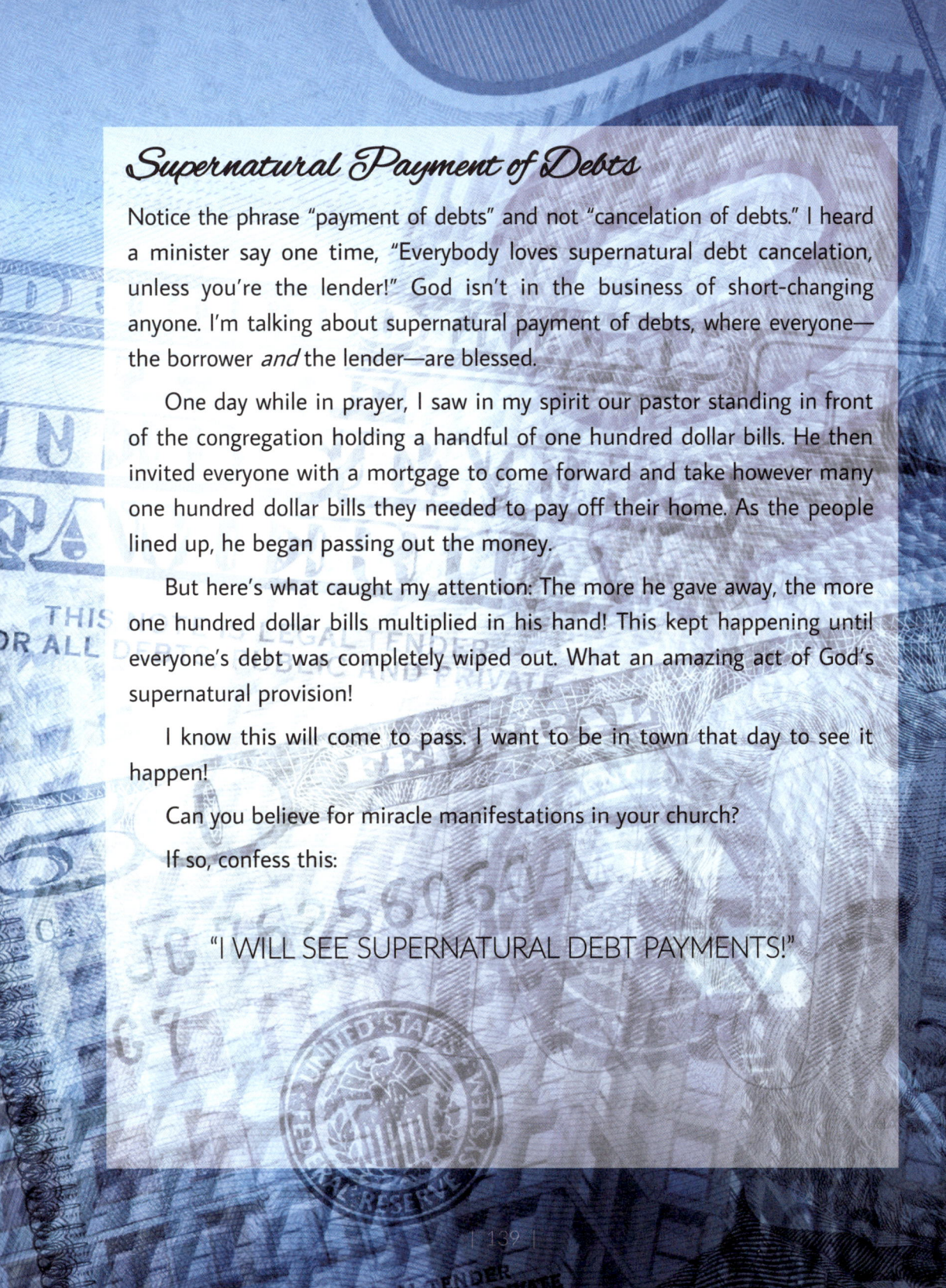

Supernatural Payment of Debts

Notice the phrase "payment of debts" and not "cancelation of debts." I heard a minister say one time, "Everybody loves supernatural debt cancelation, unless you're the lender!" God isn't in the business of short-changing anyone. I'm talking about supernatural payment of debts, where everyone—the borrower *and* the lender—are blessed.

One day while in prayer, I saw in my spirit our pastor standing in front of the congregation holding a handful of one hundred dollar bills. He then invited everyone with a mortgage to come forward and take however many one hundred dollar bills they needed to pay off their home. As the people lined up, he began passing out the money.

But here's what caught my attention: The more he gave away, the more one hundred dollar bills multiplied in his hand! This kept happening until everyone's debt was completely wiped out. What an amazing act of God's supernatural provision!

I know this will come to pass. I want to be in town that day to see it happen!

Can you believe for miracle manifestations in your church?

If so, confess this:

"I WILL SEE SUPERNATURAL DEBT PAYMENTS!"

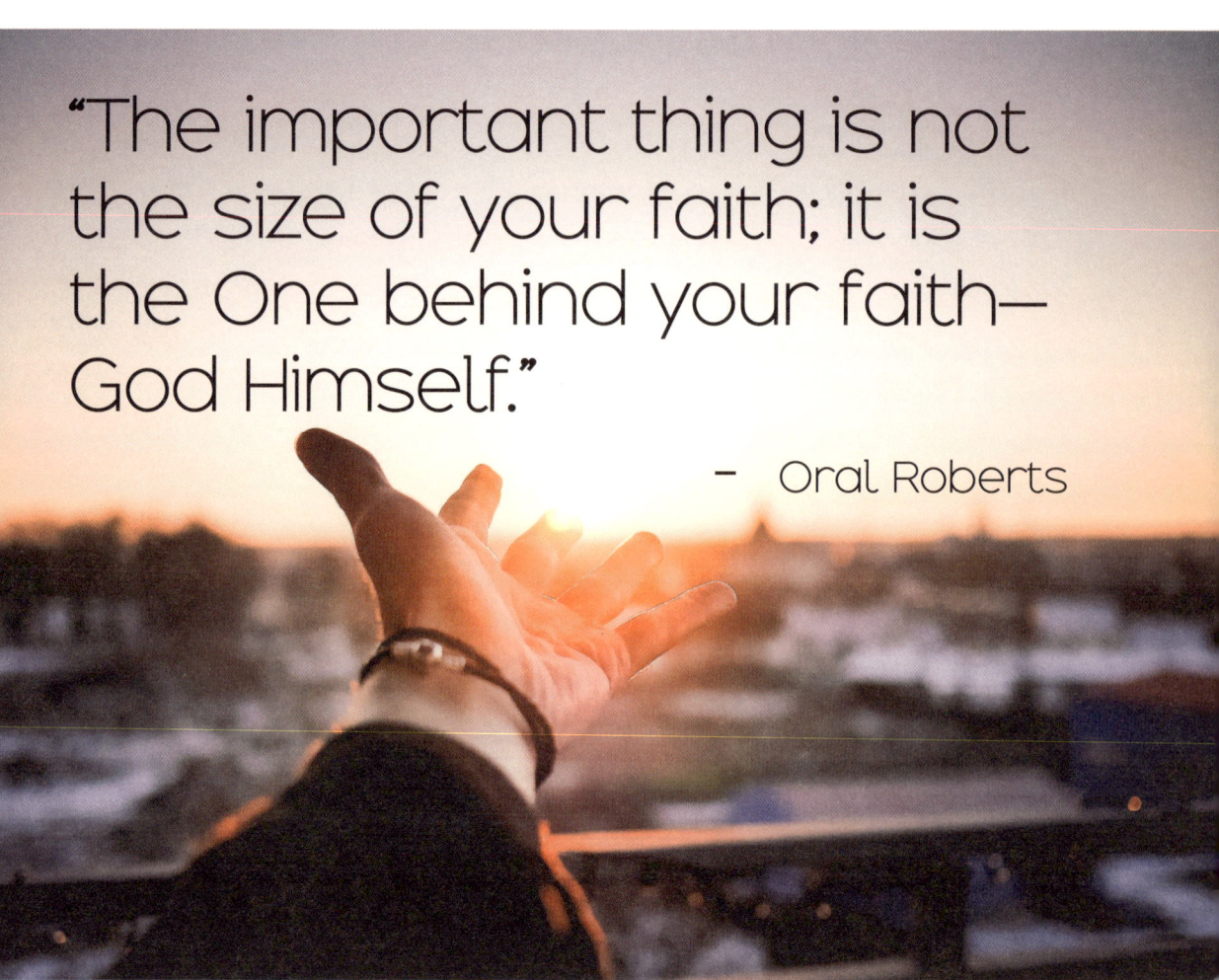

"The important thing is not the size of your faith; it is the One behind your faith— God Himself."

– Oral Roberts

Mass Resurrections

What if after a major natural catastrophe, all the dead bodies got up and started preaching about the wonders of Heaven? It could happen! Jesus raised the dead. The apostles raised the dead.

In fact, Matthew 27:52-53 records multitudes of people being raised from the dead at the same time. Talk about a witness for the Kingdom of God?

Can you believe?

If so, then confess this:

"YES, GOD, DO IT! LET US SEE RESURRECTIONS AROUND THE WORLD!"

Supernatural Weight Loss

I know someone just read this and shouted, "Yes, Lord! Do this one in me!"

Can you see a church service where everyone who needed to lose weight suddenly shrank to their ideal body size? Fifty, one hundred, two hundred pounds . . . all gone in an instant! That day is going to be so awesome! I guarantee you *that* church will be FULL the next service for sure! (Now you see why it's always good to go to church—so you don't miss any miracles!)

If you've ever been overweight, you know how difficult it is to lose weight in the natural. Most doctors give the same advice: "Eat less, drink more water, exercise more," etc.

It sounds simple, but if it was that easy, we wouldn't have so many weight issues in this country. Many people are overweight due to factors other than diet and exercise. Things like the fear of failure, the fear of abandonment, or the fear of rejection can produce a hormonal imbalance and affect the immune system. Anxiety, stress, chaos, and brokenheartedness can result in depression, insomnia, high blood pressure, high cholesterol, etc.—all which have an adverse effect on the body. If we believe that God is our Healer, then why not believe that He can completely, supernaturally transform a body?

FILLIONAIRES believe He can and He will.

I know this whole idea of supernatural weight loss might be a far-fetched concept for you to wrap your mind around, but consider how much the Bible talks about it:

* Isaiah 61:3 promises us a garment of praise instead of the SPIRIT OF HEAVINESS.

* Hebrews 12:1 says we can lay aside EVERY WEIGHT and run the race that is set before us.

* Matthew 11:28 Jesus promises us rest and release from being HEAVY LADEN.

Just take a look around you. Mass weight loss is something we desperately need in this generation!

Confess this:

"I WILL SEE SUPERNATURAL WEIGHT LOSS!"

Are You Ready?

These are only a scratch on the surface of what God wants to do in our generation. I could write an entire book on things we've never seen but will see. Sure, some of these seem out of this world. That's exactly why they're called miracles!

Our job is simply to believe and then act in faith, so God can do what He does best.

God's ready. He's been ready since Creation. The question is: Are we ready? Are we ready to experience what the disciples did?

"The crowds were stunned with bewildered wonder saying, 'Never before has anything like this been seen in Israel.'"

Matthew 9:33 (AMPC)

We need to get ready for things we've never seen before, so when they happen, we are not standing around stupefied. Rather, we can bear witness to the glory and power of our Almighty God!

For every challenge we face, God has a FAITH PERSPECTIVE that will change how we respond. Remember, we live in two realms: the natural realm, which we can see; and the unseen world, that is only visible with spiritual eyes.

Lord, open both sets of our eyes to see Your glory!

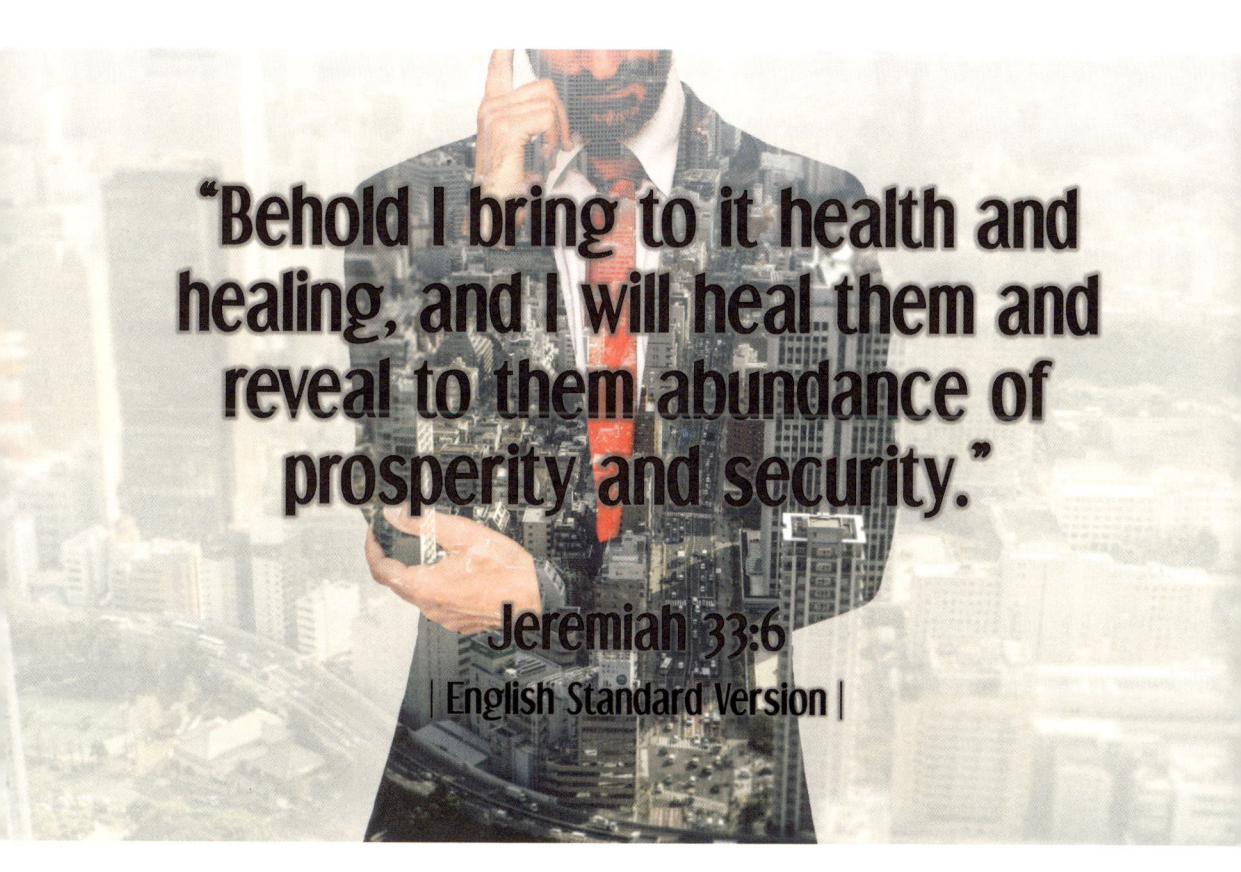

"Behold I bring to it health and healing, and I will heal them and reveal to them abundance of prosperity and security."

Jeremiah 33:6
| English Standard Version |

Secrets Revealed

There's a great example of someone's spiritual eyes being opened in 2 Kings Chapter 6.

God kept showing the prophet Elisha all the secret battle plans of Israel's enemies. Elisha knew what they were going to do, when they were going to do it, and where they planned their attack. When he told the king these revelations, Israel escaped the plots of their enemies.

The king of Syria finally figured out what was happening! He, then, ordered a great army to take out the one man who could see the unseen—Elisha. Of course, I've always wondered how this king thought he could sneak up on the guy who could see everything before it happened?

One morning, Elisha's servant got up and looked out the window. To his surprise, the entire city was surrounded by enemy horses and chariots. He must have thought, "Hey, Elisha! Why didn't God tell you about this one?" But Elisha already knew what to do.

To stop the servant's panic, Elisha replied:

"Stop being afraid, because there are more with us than with them."

2 Kings 6:16 (ISV)

Then, Elisha prayed that God would open his servant's eyes. When he looked again, he saw a completely different scenario. This time, the servant saw what Elisha saw: the mountains full of angelic chariots of fire surrounding the entire army of the enemy.

His perspective had drastically changed. What happened next is even more amazing.

Elisha prayed, and the entire Syrian army went totally blind. Then, he led them all into the center of Samaria's town square, where he then prayed for God to open their eyes.

Boy, were they surprised! They were completely surrounded by the armies of Israel, ready to take them all down.

But, God had another plan.

The king of Israel asked Elisha if they should kill the Syrians. God said, "No." Instead, they threw a feast, fed their enemies, and sent them back home. Israel never heard from them again!

What this story teaches us is simple: FILLIONAIRES need to pray bold prayers, prayers that reach beyond our natural realm and into the unseen world of the spirit—God's world, to be exact. Then, we will clearly know the plans of God and will be at the right place at the right time, doing the right thing!

Are you ready?

Put it to Work

Faith for the unseen, supernatural works of God is great, but the Bible says it's entirely fruitless without corresponding action. Faith without works is dead. (See James 2:26.)

You build your faith every time you use your God-given, sanctified imagination to envision miracles of healing, provision, and signs and wonders that show how great your God is!

Start imagining the impossible happening all around you—in your family, church, business, etc. Don't limit God.

Cyndy and I do this on a very regular basis.

My wife loves to take pictures and document memories. Many times, she takes her camera to church. You may be asking, "Why would anyone take a camera to church?" Well, I can guarantee you it's not so she can take pictures of the latest church fashion trends. No, she's on a mission to see the unseen.

Cyndy isn't looking to capture what she can see, rather she's taking pictures, hoping to capture things she can't see like angelic activity in the room that no one else sees. Many times, we look through her pictures, completely expecting to see angels in the room.

It's time to put our faith to work by thinking, praying, and believing for these things.

People who are watching or streaming our church services are seeing angels that no one present in the services sees. The windows of heaven are opening up, so we can see what God sees.

Then, as we begin to testify of the miracle power of God at work, God confirms it with instant signs and wonders.

Prepare your heart and eyes to believe and see the supernatural things God wants to do. Tell your body to get ready. Develop your faith every single day. God's will is simple: to live a supernatural life, so we can bring Him all the glory!

IT'S CALLED LIVING THE FILLIONAIRE LIFE!

Fillionaire
STRATEGIES
#6

. . . FOR SEEING THE UNSEEN!

* Think outside your faith box.
* Expect something supernatural to happen to you today.
* Pay attention to your spirit.
* Pray with a new mindset of faith.
* Receive new eyes and a new vision.

DECLARE THIS:

"I have the ability to think outside of the box!"

"And you've become a new person. This new person is continually renewed in knowledge to be like its creator." (Colossians 3:10, GW)

"I expect something supernatural to happen to me today!"

"Everyone around was in awe—all those wonders and signs done through the apostles! And all the believers lived in a wonderful harmony, holding everything in common. They sold whatever they owned and pooled their resources so that each person's need was met." (Acts 2:43-45, MSG)

"I pay close attention to what the Holy Spirit is showing me!"

"So we have the prophetic word strongly confirmed. You will do well to pay attention to it, as to a lamp shining in a dismal place, until the day dawns and the morning star rises in your hearts." (2 Peter 1:19, HCSB)

"I pray my way into a new mindset of faith!"

"So we keep on praying for you, asking our God to enable you to live a life worthy of his call. May he give you the power to accomplish all the good things your faith prompts you to do." (2 Thessalonians 1:11, NLT)

"I receive new eyes and a new vision for the supernatural!"

"The message of one who hears the words of God, who has knowledge from the Most High, who sees a vision from the Almighty, who bows down with eyes wide open:" (Numbers 24:16, NLT)

Wake Up Younger

It's amazing the things you hear standing in the checkout line at the store. One particular conversation stands out in my mind.

There I was, simply waiting to pay for my stuff, when two ladies struck up a conversation with the checkout clerk. One lady commented that her eyesight had weakened since she turned forty years old. The other two chimed in, adding their own thoughts on the inevitability of growing older.

Standing there in line, these three ladies began comparing all their aches, pains, and age-induced conditions. For a minute, I thought I was in a drug commercial listening to all the side effects. Their various conditions weren't what grabbed my attention, but rather that they all fully expected their health to deteriorate as they grew older.

I decline to agree with their failing-health philosophy. Instead, I've decided to believe what the Bible says, that I wake up younger every day!

Many people use age as an excuse as to why their bodies are falling apart and their minds are not properly functioning but not FILLIONAIRES! We think differently. We live according to Psalms 103:5, that says God's power and His presence renews our youth like the eagles . . .

. . . every single day.

My last well-check doctor's visit was quite the experience. Every

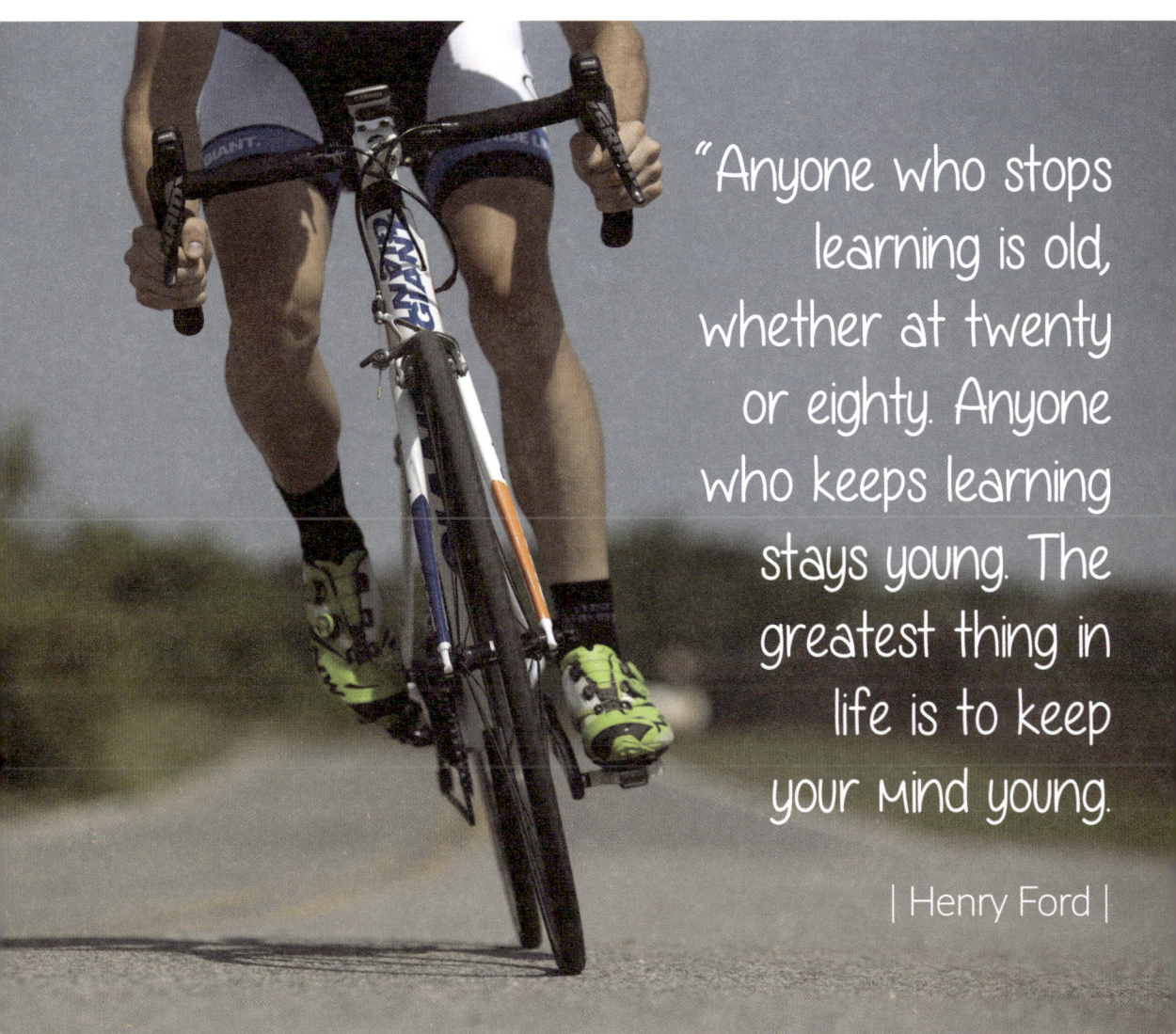

"Anyone who stops learning is old, whether at twenty or eighty. Anyone who keeps learning stays young. The greatest thing in life is to keep your mind young.

| Henry Ford |

nurse who bounded through the door made their entrance by happily announcing their name. "Hi, I'm Debbie," said the first nurse. The one right behind her declared, "I'm Tammy!" Another one burst in and said, "Good morning! I'm Sally." (The names have been changed to protect the innocent!) Their positive and upbeat attitude was amazing, especially since they were only there to take my blood pressure, check my temperature, and listen to my heart rate. To them, it was the best job in the universe.

As they combed through my chart to confirm all the information, one of the nurses commented, "Mr. Nordyke, it seems you only use a nose spray for allergies and take vitamins. Is this correct?" "Yes,

ma'am," I responded. She continued, "But your blood pressure and heart rate are so good," "That's right," I said. "It's because I wake up younger every day!"

That became the catch phrase for my entire visit.

The nurse needing to draw blood said, "You have good veins." The others then replied, "That's because he wakes up younger every day!" This continued the remainder of my visit.

Afterwards, I thought, *"Wow, how refreshing that all the nurses got involved with God's age-reversal plan for me!"*

Maybe being a FILLIONAIRE is contagious!

"He renews your youth—you're always young in His presence."

Psalms 103:5b

| The Message Bible |

Stretch!

Okay, the youth renewal mindset may be stretching your faith a bit. I hope it is! That's the purpose of this book. But, just so you know, this isn't something I dreamed up on my own. Here are a few scriptures that promise a youth renewal anointing:

You can live vigorous.

> "Refreshed, His eyes lit up with renewed vigor!"
>
> 1 Samuel 14:27 (MSG)

You can live fresh.

> "My glory and honor are [resh in me [being constantly renewed], and bow gains [ever] new strength in my hand."
>
> Job 29:20 (AMPC)

You can live youthful.

> "Let their flesh be renewed like a child's, let them be restored as in the days of their youth."
>
> Job 33:25 (NIV)

celebrated

You can live completely satisfied.

"Who satisfies your mouth [your necessity at your personal age and situation] with good, so that your youth, renewed, is like the eagle's [strong, overcoming, soaring]."

Psalms 103:5 (AMPC)

You can live renewed.

"Behold, I long for your precepts; in your righteousness give me renewed life."

Psalms 119:40 (AMPC)

You can live strong.

"But those who wait for the Lord [who expect, look for and hope in Him] shall change and renew their strength and power; they shall lift their wings and mount up [close to God] as eagles [mount up to the sun] they shall run and not be weary, they shall walk and not faint or become tired."

Isaiah 40:31 (AMPC)

● ● ● ● ● ● ● ● ● ● ● ● ● ●

You can live celebrated.

"The Lord your God is with you. He is a hero who saves you. He happily rejoices over you, renews you with His love and celebrates over you with shouts of joy."

Zephaniah 3:17 (GW)

You can live transformed and changed.

". . . in view of [all] the mercies of God. Make a decisive dedication of your bodies [presenting all your members and faculties] as a living sacrifice. . . . Do NOT be conformed to this world, . . . but be transformed [changed] by the entire renewal of your mind . . ."

Romans 12:1-2 (AMPC)

You can live regenerated.

"And be constantly renewed in the spirit of your mind [having a fresh mental and spiritual attitude] and put on the new nature [the regenerated self] created in God's image, [Godlike] in true righteousness and holiness."

Ephesians 4:23-24 (AMPC)

YOUNGER

| young • er |

YOUTHFUL, FRESH, VIGOROUS.

What Young People Do

One of the greatest examples of someone who lived this type of youth-renewed life is God's best friend, Abraham. The older he became, the younger he lived!

When Abraham was seventy-five years old, God told him, "Hey, let's run away from home and backpack Europe!" Now, that's not what normal, responsible seventy-five-year-old people do, right?

That's what young people do.

Then, twenty-five years later, God told Abraham, "I want to bless you with a baby." That's not what someone who has reached the century mark does—not to mention his wife, Sarah, was ninety!

That's what young people do.

But Abraham and Sarah got together and had a baby boy. The whole thought of someone their age having a baby had to be hilarious. Maybe that's why they named their son, "Isaac," which means, "laughter!"

When Isaac turned twelve and his dad was one hundred and twelve, God came up with another great idea: "Abraham, take your son mountain climbing! I want to show you something really cool."

Wait a minute.

Mountain climbing?

With a twelve year-old boy?

That's what young people do, right? Abraham was just getting started.

After Sarah passed away at the age of one hundred and twenty-six, Abraham got married again to a lady named Keturah, and they had six more kids! Here's Abraham at one hundred and forty having more children!

That's what young people do.

Abraham lived to be a hundred and seventy-five years old, which means he followed God for one hundred years. How was he able to leave his country, his father, and his children and go climb mountains and lead a nation—all while over the age of seventy-five?

Easy.

It's what young people do.

The Seed

Most people who know the biblical account of Abraham think it's a nice story—and, it is—but it's far more than just one man's journey of faith.

Abraham's life is the prototype for his seed—FILLIONAIRES like you and me!

● ● ● ● ● ● ● ● ● ● ● ●

BECAUSE OF THIS PROMISE FROM GOD, WE CAN LIVE AND FUNCTION AS YOUNGER PEOPLE, NO MATTER WHAT OUR AGE!

● ● ● ● ● ● ● ● ● ● ● ●

The Bible says we are the seed of Abraham (See Galatians 3:29.) and *all* of His blessings belong to us! (See Galatians 3:14.)

How many of His blessings?

All of them—including youth renewal!

Because of this promise from God, we can live and function as younger people, no matter what our age! God is no respecter of persons. He doesn't play favorites. What He granted to Abraham, He will do for anyone who believes.

What this means to me is quite simply this: I wake up younger every day!

Begin surrounding yourself with things that accentuate your new, young life. Replace pictures of you

being old with ones that show your youth. Don't walk around saying, "I'm getting old." Instead, say what God says about you: "My youth is renewed. I wake up younger every day!" Feed your faith, and thank God for His divine youth-renewal plan.

FILLIONAIRE, you are the seed of Abraham! Youthfulness is promised to you throughout your entire life. Through being full of God's Word and His glory, you have the capacity to rejuvenate your cells and be renewed in your body and mind. If you need healing, Jesus has already provided it. If you need finances to eat correctly, Jesus has already provided it. If it's your memory that needs to be renewed, He has the power to renew your mind.

You have a race to run and a heavenly assignment to accomplish. It's time to take your youthfulness by faith and enjoy strength, health, and energy like never before! You are as young as you believe you are. Age is simply a number. Renew your mind. Believe and confess:

"I WAKE UP YOUNGER EVERY DAY."

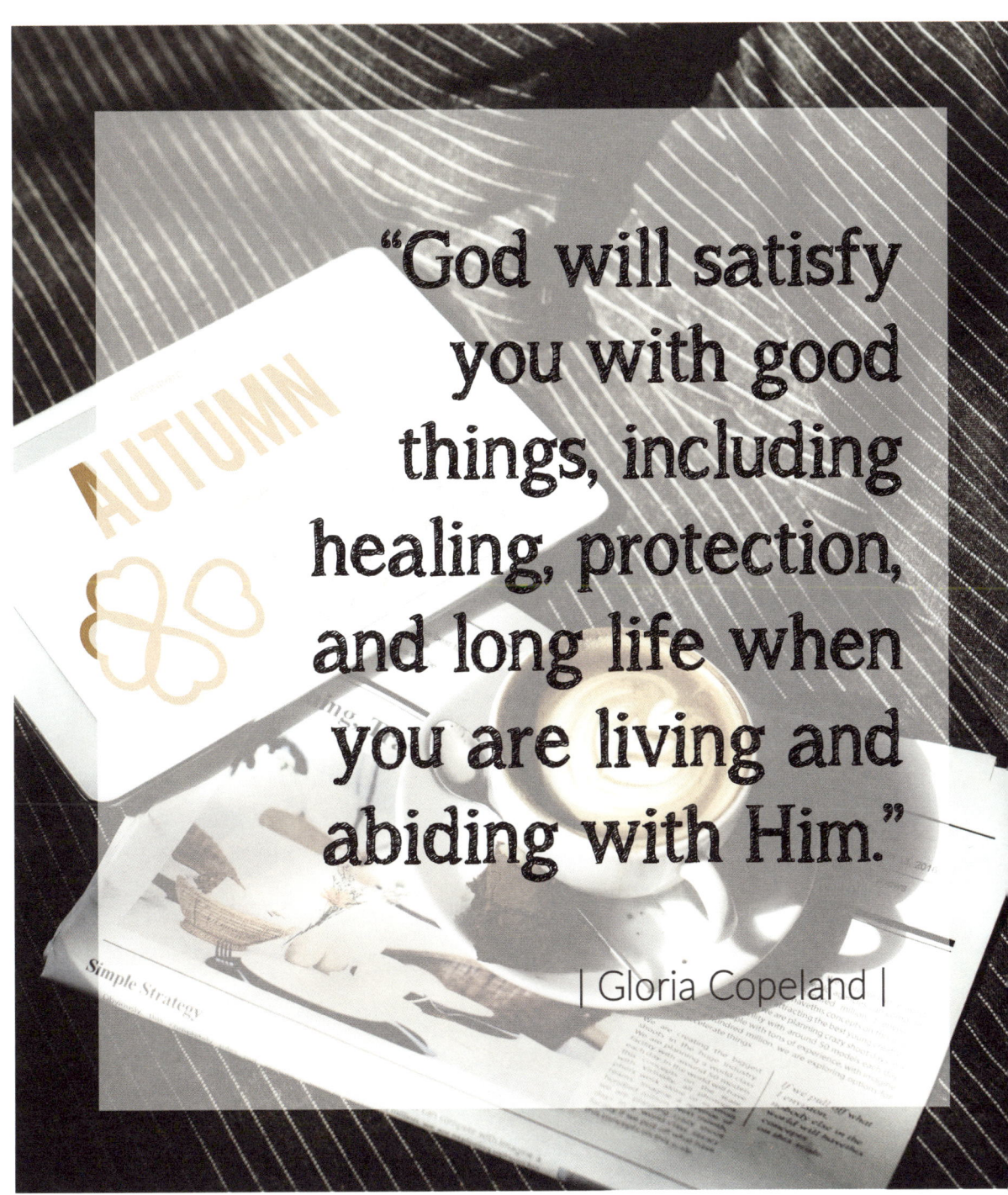

"God will satisfy you with good things, including healing, protection, and long life when you are living and abiding with Him."

| Gloria Copeland |

Fillionaire STRATEGIES #7

. . . FOR WAKING UP YOUNGER EVERYDAY

* Change your "OLD" talk into "NEW" talk.
* Think outside your natural conditions.
* Live in child-like faith.
* Do what young people do.
* Enjoy life, and be full of energy.
* Love yourself, and love what God is doing.

DECLARE THESE:

"I change my 'old' talk into 'new' talk!"

"He who was seated on the throne said, 'I am making everything new!' Then he said, 'Write this down, for these words are trustworthy and true.'" (Revelation 21:5, NIV)

"I live in the faith of a child!"

"To Titus, my true child after a common faith: Grace and peace from God the Father and Christ Jesus our Savior." (Titus 1:4, NASB)

"I do what young people do!"

"So David sent ten young men; and David said to the young men, 'Go up to Carmel and go to Nabal, and greet him in my name; and this is what you shall say, "Have a long life! Peace be to you, and peace to your house, and peace to all that you have." (1 Samuel 25:5-6, AMPC)

"I enjoy life, and I'm full of energy!"

"Do it with all the strength and energy that God supplies. Then everything you do will bring glory to God through Jesus Christ. All glory and power to him forever and ever! Amen." (1 Peter 4:11b, NLT)

"I love myself, and I love what God is doing in me!"

"Righteous Father, although the world has not known You, I know You, and they know that You sent Me. And I have made Your name known to them and will continue to make it known, so that the love You have for Me may be in them, and I in them." (John 17:25-26, BSB)

Immeasurable

CHAPTER 8

*C*yndy and I have always traveled our entire married life. One valuable lesson we've learned over the years is to take time for visiting cool places while on these journeys.

While on a trip to California to minister for our good friends, Rocky and Jean Tannehill, they took us to visit The Hearst Castle. The castle was designed and built by William Randolph Hearst, one of multi-millionaires George and Phoebe Hearst's five sons. At ten years old, William visited Europe with his mother, where he fell in love with the architecture and majesty of the buildings—and the seed was planted. It was then that young William determined to construct a palace of such beauty and magnitude for his own enjoyment—and that he did!

When we arrived, we were surprised to see there were several tours to choose from. Each one took over an hour to complete, and no one tour showed the entire property. We quickly understood why: It was larger than life! Just look at some of its features:

* 56 bedrooms
* 61 bathrooms
* 19 sitting rooms
* 90,000 square feet of living space
* A 127-acre garden

* Indoor and outdoor swimming pools
* Tennis courts
* A full-size movie theater
* An airfield for guests to land their private planes

I'd say William knew a thing or two about extravagance!

The castle's sprawling exterior was complimented by its pristine, luxurious interior. Priceless artifacts collected over twenty-eight years, from exquisite European cathedrals to ancient Egyptian pyramids, filled every room and hallway.

Proud to display their massive fortune, the Hearsts were known to throw outlandish parties for Hollywood's A-list actors and actresses and the day's social icons, which included Charlie Chaplain, Cary Grant, and

IMMEASURABLE

| im • meas • ur • a • ble |

IMMENSE; INDEFINITELY EXTENSIVE; NOT TO BE MEASURED; BEYOND ALL MEASURE.

Clark Gable. President Franklin D. Roosevelt and Sir Winston Churchill also stayed at the castle.

Cyndy and I just walked around in awe, amazed at the mansion's opulence. The stories and history of each tapestry, fireplace, and pool-side statue were overwhelmingly inspiring. Towards the end of the tour, we heard the most astonishing fact: That magnificent castle—with its over-the-top architecture and fine collection of artifacts—wasn't even William Hearst's main home! It was his summer cottage!

Wow! Now, I was officially over-whelmed.

Hearing that one amazing fact stretched my thinking and imagi-nation beyond anything I had ever experienced up to that time.

All these rooms full of priceless art, books, rugs, and sculptures—all purchased for the sole purpose of his pure enjoyment! Undoubtedly, William Hearst reached a level of success very few others enjoyed at that time . . .

. . . and he knew how to live like a FILLIONAIRE—immeasurably!

Yes, even though The Hearst Castle was unbelievable; compared to Heaven, it's just a tiny house! In Heaven, the streets are made of gold; giant gates are made from a single, massive pearl; the mansions are as far as the eye can see; and precious stones and flawless gems cover the walls—all displaying the Kingdom of God's immeasurable resources.

And just as Mr. Hearst invited the rich and famous of his day to come and enjoy his creation, our Heavenly Father is calling us to live in a new level of faith:

* A level where miracles abound and bodies are supernaturally healed.

* A level where needs disappear.

* A level where the impossible becomes possible.

* A level of endless provision.

He's calling us to live the FILLIONAIRE life!

Even though they lived in luxury, the Hearst's riches (along with everyone else who has ever lived on this planet) are measurable. Someone can calculate what they're worth—NOT so with the Kingdom of God! It's too much to measure. One word best describes God's riches:

Immeasurable!

The story of Joseph is a perfect example.

Gather it Up

While Joseph was imprisoned (for something he didn't do), Pharaoh had two dreams. Now, these weren't your normal, run-of-the-mill dreams; they included very specific characters which represented a very specific meaning.

Pharaoh saw himself standing by a river when all of a sudden, seven fat, healthy cows came out of the water, followed by seven skinny, ugly cows. As the fat cows grazed in the meadow, the skinny ones came and ate them alive. Definitely weird! But, that was just the beginning.

Pharaoh's second dream was along the same lines. Seven heads of plump grain were devoured by seven skinny heads. Little did he know the prophetic forecast he was seeing.

After his chief magicians could not interpret these dreams, Pharaoh learned of Joseph's ability to interpret dreams and summoned him from prison.

Upon hearing Pharaoh's dreams, Joseph began unpacking the true meaning of the prophetic dreams, which foretold the next fourteen years of Egypt's future. Pharaoh honored Joseph by appointing him second in command in what was considered the greatest nation of its time.

During the first seven years—the years of abundance—Joseph was responsible for overseeing all of Egypt's food production. Knowing that seven years of famine were coming, they saved as much as they could, and God blessed it. The Bible says it like this:

"Joseph gathered very much grain, as the sand of the sea, until he stopped counting, for it was IMMEASURABLE."

Genesis 41:49 (NKJV)

I love that phrase: "until he stopped counting." Imagine being given the task of counting the grains of sand.

It's IMMEASURABLE!

Joseph gathered and gathered . . . and gathered and gathered, until he could no longer count it. How much did he gather?

An immeasurable amount!

That sounds like the nature of God to me!

How much does He desire to bless you? *Beyond your ability to measure it!*

The Key

God is an immeasurable God. You and I cannot measure His love, His goodness, or His desire to do awesome miracles for His children. The problem isn't the source; it's the receiving end—us!

Do we see God like He really is? Do we believe God desires to lavish His endless riches upon us?

Our faith holds the key.

I've never met anyone who didn't know what it felt like to be limited. Whether it's finances, time, energy, resources, opportunities, etc.—we all have dealt with limitations.

But, when it comes to dealing with limitations, here's the truth:

• • • • • • • • • • •

LIMITATIONS ARE NOTHING MORE THAN FAITH BORDERS.

• • • • • • • • • • •

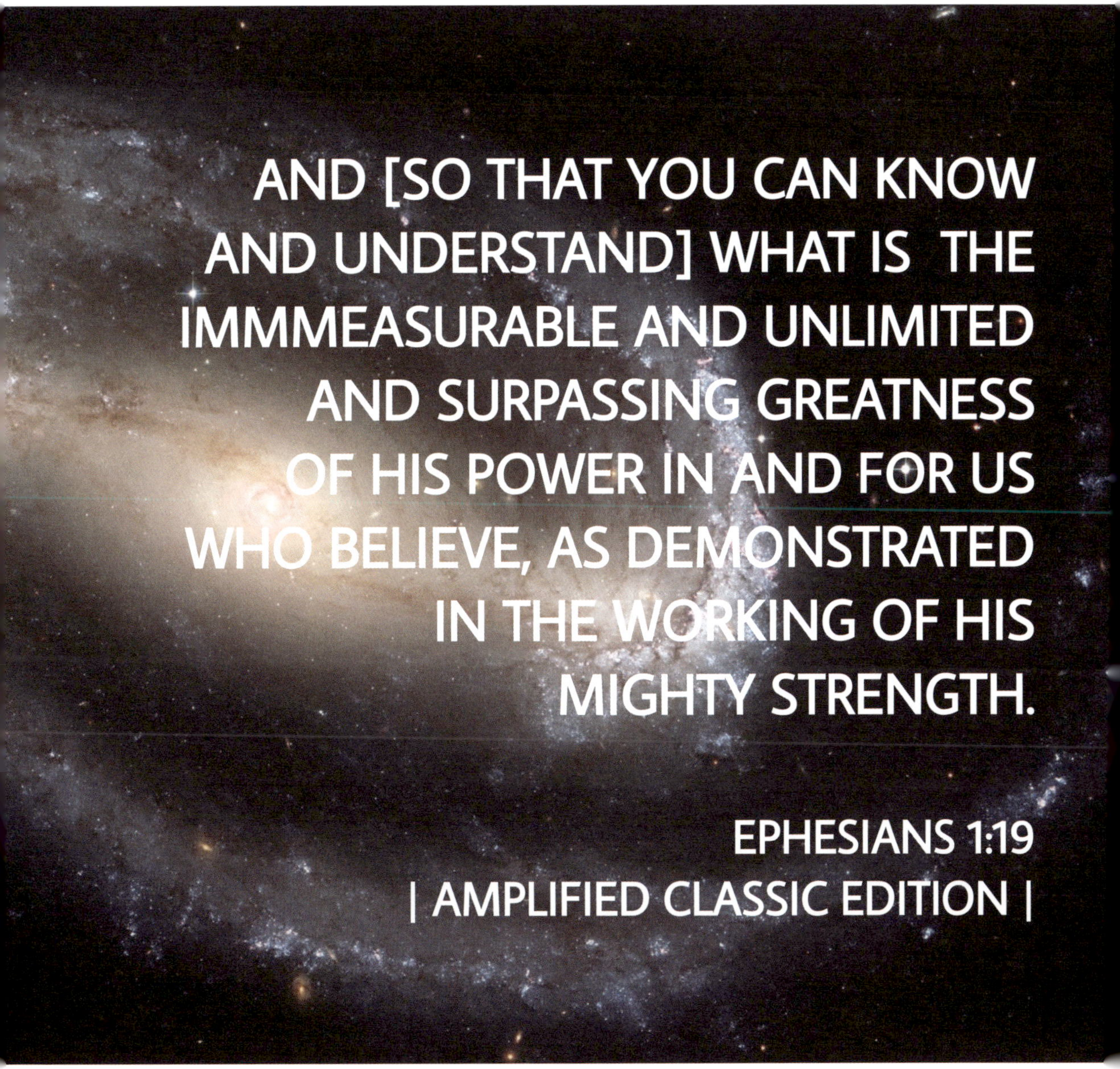

AND [SO THAT YOU CAN KNOW
AND UNDERSTAND] WHAT IS THE
IMMMEASURABLE AND UNLIMITED
AND SURPASSING GREATNESS
OF HIS POWER IN AND FOR US
WHO BELIEVE, AS DEMONSTRATED
IN THE WORKING OF HIS
MIGHTY STRENGTH.

EPHESIANS 1:19
| AMPLIFIED CLASSIC EDITION |

If Mark 9:23 is right and all things are truly possible to him who believes, then why do we have areas in our hearts where our faith stops working? Can't we go beyond natural limitations, step into a new realm, and walk where Jesus walked . . . on the water?

The answer is a resounding, "Yes!"

Faith holds the key.

On many occasions, Jesus taught people, "According to your faith, be it unto you!" (See Matthew 9:22, 29; 15:28, and 17:20.) The same principle is true today. What limits do you need to break through? What are you stretching your faith for? What are you believing God to do? His supply is immeasurable. If you can believe it, you can have it.

Your miracles are not dependent upon your abilities, resources, or connections. Your level of miracles relies on your willingness to believe beyond the natural and into the supernatural. Everyone who believed Jesus was the "One sent from God" experienced miracles.

Now, it's your turn.

Use your key.

Use your faith to see His great love towards you. See how He loves to heal you, how He loves to provide for you, how He loves to bless you. Don't allow wrong thinking to take you out of your miracle flow. If you think God is constantly mad at you, your faith will be severely hindered. Thoughts of unworthiness undermine the power of His great love which has forgiven all your sin. If you are always counting your good works or bad works, stop it! Stop counting now! That's a *limited* number. Move your thoughts from the finite to the infinite, from the restricted to the endless, from the measurable to God's realm:

IMMEASURABLE!

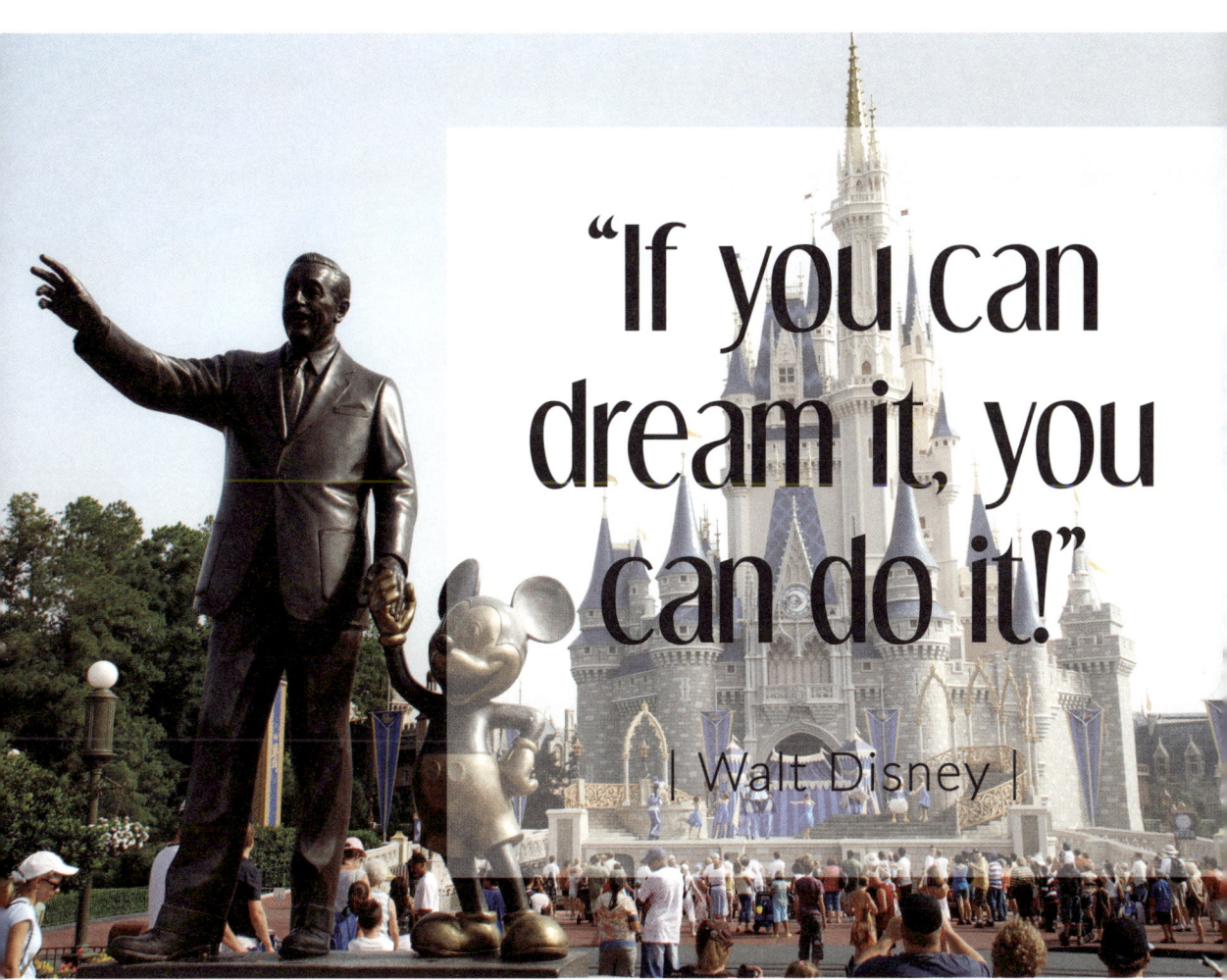

"If you can dream it, you can do it!"

| Walt Disney |

Rise Up

What do you need from God? Tell Him; He already knows anyways. He's just waiting for you to take the time and talk to Him. While you're there, ask Him what He wants to tell you, show you, or do inside your heart. You might be surprised what happens when you move into His realm—the realm of the immeasurable!

Once you step into a flow of faith that removes all limits, you will find yourself experiencing more miracles that you can count.

It's the life of a FILLIONAIRE.

Instead of trying to just pay your bills, imagine being positioned by God to influence and bless entire nations! Imagine being able to solve the whole world's problems, just because you used your faith and believed.

Psalms 2:8 talks about this type of life:

> *"Ask of Me, and I will give you the nations for your inheritance, and the ends of the earth for your possession."*
>
> **(AMPC)**

Make the decision to live with no limitations. Rise up and live in the miracle realm God has already promised you in His Word. His grace towards you is immeasurable, His love for you is immeasurable, and His plan for your life is also immeasurable. God has an unlimited supply, and His power and ability is limitless.

Fillionaire
STRATEGIES #8

. . . FOR LIVING IMMEASURABLY!

* Think bigger.
* Pray bigger than you think.
* Believe bigger than you pray.
* Get your confession in line with immeasurable results.
* Act like God is your dad.
* Live greatly!

DECLARE THESE:

"I think bigger than ever before!"

"I will surely bless you, and I will surely multiply your offspring as the stars of heaven and as the sand that is on the seashore. And your offspring shall possess the gate of his enemies." (Genesis 22:17, ESV)

"I pray bigger than I can think!"

". . . The heavens are telling of the glory of God; and their expanse is declaring the work of His hands. Day to day pours forth speech, and night to night reveals knowledge." (Psalms 19:1-2, NASB)

"I believe bigger than I pray!"

"Praise him in his mighty acts; praise him according to the abundance of his greatness." (Psalms 150:2, DBY)

"I line my faith up with God's immeasurable ability!"

"And what is the immeasurable greatness of his power toward us who believe, according to the working of his great might." (Ephesians 1:19, ESV)

"I am the revival!

"Give thanks to the Lord. Call on His name. Make known among the nations what He has done." (Psalms 105:1, GW)

CHAPTER 9

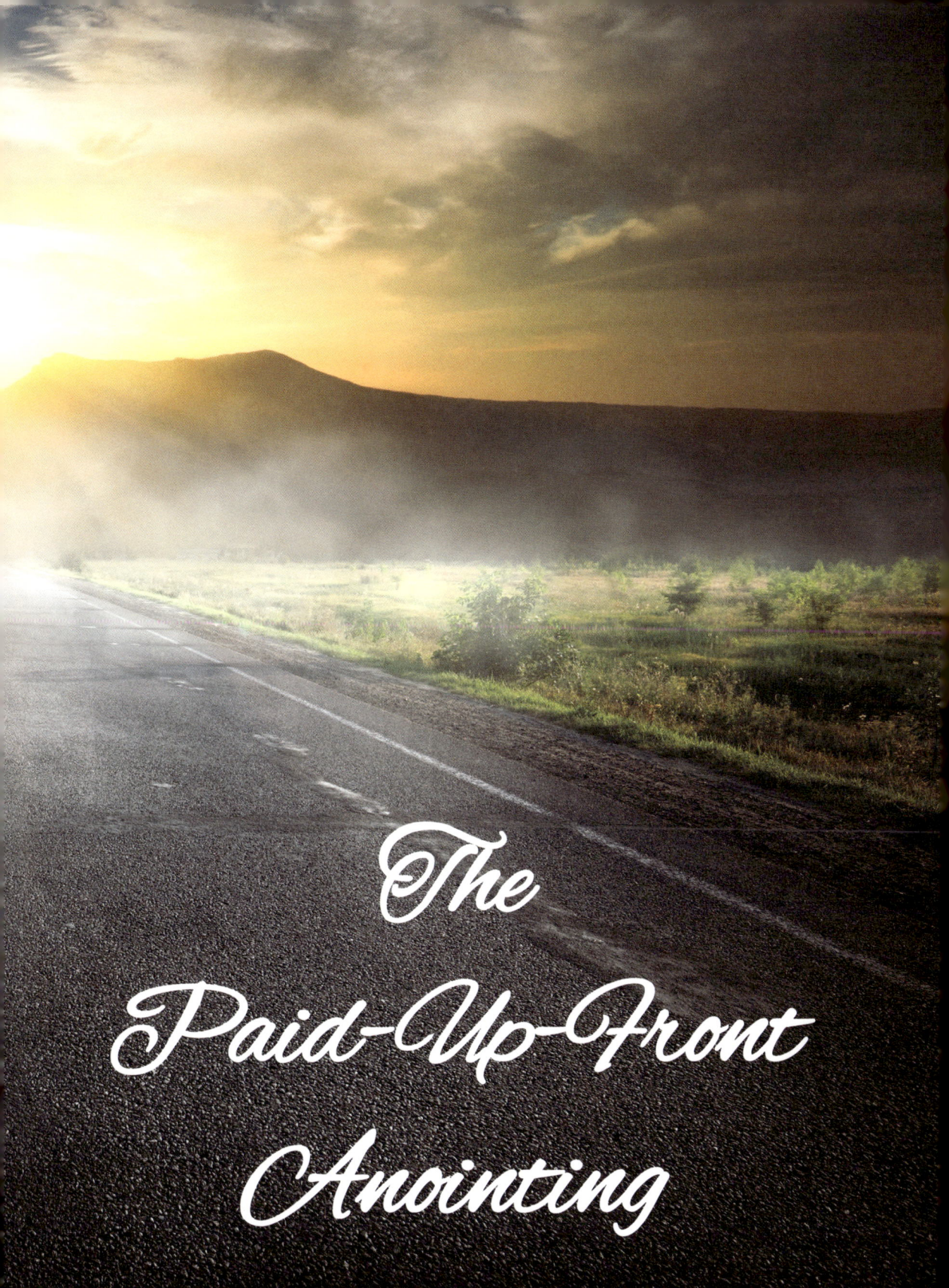

The Paid-Up-Front Anointing

S unday, January 8, 2017. You can only guess what Cyndy and I were doing that morning: driving to church.

And what were we doing?

You got it—praying, as usual.

While praying in the Spirit, I began to declare these words:

"THE PAID-UP-FRONT ANOINTING IS BEING MANIFESTED FOR THE REVIVAL CAPITAL OF THE WORLD!"

As far as I can remember, I've never said nor heard anyone else say the phrase: "paid-up-front-anointing." Once again, God had my attention.

That morning, Pastor Pearsons brought an amazing message called, "A Year of Great Prosperity." It was an awesome beginning-of-the-year challenge to the Body of Christ to believe God to pour out His BIG blessings, so we can fulfill His BIG plans for revival in our generation. The message was timely and crucial for the day and time in which we live.

One of the stories Pastor George shared that morning was how he and Pastor Terri became debt-free concerning their home. While relating how they renovated their house, he said, "We paid as we went."

As soon as he said this, something immediately rose up in my heart, and I heard in my spirit:

"THE PAID-UP-FRONT ANOINTING IS NOW RELEASED!"

The power of God was on me so strong; I could hardly sit still in my seat.

Pastor George began sharing the vision for the airplanes they were believing God for, the 10,000-seat auditorium they were taking by faith, and the 50,000-seater auditorium that would follow.

As he spoke, I could feel the FILLIONAIRE anointing fill the entire place. It seemed as though nothing was impossible!

The truth is, it's all possible—and we're going to see it all come to pass with our very own eyes. It's time for the paid-up-front anointing to take over, which will allow us to pay for everything in advance!

"You Have Until Friday"

While asking the Lord what the meaning was of this phrase, He reminded me of an incident we experienced some years ago.

In 1996, Cyndy and I planted an independent church, Youth WAVE Church, and pastored it for ten years. During that time, it came to our attention that there were many high school students in our area who wanted to graduate but needed an alternative method. We did our research and then agreed to host a Texas charter school called Youth WAVE High School.

Cyndy served as the principal, overseeing all the daily operations and more than twenty-five full-time staff members, along with taking care of about two hundred students. It was a huge learning experience, to say the least. One thing she quickly realized was how much government money is invested every year in our education system.

One Tuesday, Cyndy received a call from the superintendent of our school district. He told her, "Cyndy you have $50,000 to spend on the technology department for your campus; but you must spend it all by Friday, or you will lose it!" Cyndy was overwhelmed! Needless to say, we immediately started looking for computers. By Friday afternoon, all the computers and software we needed were purchased—bought and paid for . . . IN FULL! Our students reaped the benefits, and our staff members were so excited!

That's called, "Paid-up-front!"

Imagine if someone called you and gave you $50,000, and then said it had to be spent by the end of the week? I can see you doing the happy dance right now! Just think of all the bills you could pay off, the car you could buy, or the new wardrobe that would be hanging in your closet. How would that make you feel? Happy? Relieved? Blessed? Prosperous?

You had better get ready. It's called the paid-up-front anointing, and it's being released right now!

Getting those computers was truly a paid-up-front experience, and Cyndy had a blast buying them! Who wouldn't have? The provision was there for a specific purpose with our school's name on it—and we spent it all!

Think about this. If a natural source can offer such an awesome, natural provision, just think what God can do in the supernatural!

I wonder how many times God has prepared similar situations for us in the faith realm? How many times has God said, "Go to this place, speak to this person, and then pray for them," but we hesitated and missed a blessing? Who knows? It could have been a divine opportunity to connect with someone or something that would eventually be a key piece to fulfilling our destiny.

Everything you need to accomplish a specific purpose, God has already provided. It has your name on it and is set aside for your use only. When you approach each day with a readiness and anticipation to receive, then miracles of provision flow. The Bible says:

PAID-UP-FRONT
| paid-up-front |

SUPPLIED IN ADVANCE; MONEY IN THE BANK; FURNISHED BEFOREHAND.

"Those who love me inherit wealth. I fill their treasuries."

Proverbs 8:21 (NLT)

God has connections, provisions, and doors of influence that He desires to open for us.

But, what if—like the money Cyndy was given for the computers that had to be used by Friday—there was a time limit to spend it? That's the time to use strong faith to access the portals of destiny and utilize the resources God has set aside for us now.

Filling ourselves with His Word builds and stretches our faith to where we can move into the spirit realm and believe God.

It's the life of a FILLIONAIRE!

"God's Kingdom is never downsizing."

| Pastor George Pearsons |

Tons and Tons

I'm telling you, the paid-up-front anointing is a real thing We see it in operation in 1 Chronicles 22:14, where King David unveiled something to his son, Solomon, who would soon become king.

"Now, look, I have made every effort to supply what is needed to build the Lord's Temple. I have stored up 100,000 talents of gold, 1,000,000 talents of silver, and so much bronze and iron it cannot be weighed, as well as wood and stones. Feel free to add more."

(NET)

God's Word Translation says it this way: *"7,500,000 pounds of gold, 75,000,000 pounds of silver."*

The New Living Bible translation describes the amount as: *"4,000 tons of gold, 40,000 tons of silver."*

Just exactly how much is this?

TONS.

THOUSANDS OF TONS.

HUNDREDS OF THOUSANDS OF TONS.

IMMEASURABLE TONS!

If you thought God only has a ton of blessings for you, think bigger!

He LOVES you tons!

He PROVIDES tons!

He has tons of MIRACLES for you!

He has stored up tons of BLESSINGS for you!

In 1 Chronicles 22:16, it goes on to say:

". . . of gold and silver and bronze there is no limit. Arise and begin working, and the Lord be with you."

(NKJV)

I love it when someone says, "The Lord be with you." To me, that's like saying:

"Let there be MIRACLES!"

"Let there be PROVISION!"

"Let there be SUCCESS and FULFILLMENT!"

Who wouldn't want to live like that every day?

FILLIONAIRES do!

If we will believe with God, for what God wants, then we can have the miracles of God. Whatever we need is supplied before we begin.

It's called the paid-up-front anointing!

Jehovah Jireh

God Knows

About five years ago, our son, Ryan, and his wife, Kathryn, were drawn to the ministry of Pastor Bill Johnson at Bethel Church in Redding, California. They really desired to be part of that ministry, so they believed God for Ryan to get hired there. Ryan, who has a great eye for graphic arts and design, applied for a web designer's position and got the job.

Right after their third child, Ethan, was born, Ryan and Kathryn packed up everything they owned and moved to California. They quickly fell in love with everything—the opportunity to work with a ministry that is impacting the world, the Redding area, and the Bethel church community. Plus, Ryan loved his job. The icing on the cake was that his office, at the time, was in the same building as the offices of Jesus Culture. They both felt so blessed.

A few years went by, and Kathryn gave birth to their fourth child, Wesley. The increase in their family

also meant an increase in expenses, so Ryan took on some side jobs from several design companies. One of these organizations really loved his artistic flair and eventually offered him a full-time position, one that paid very well and allowed him more time to spend with his growing family. The amazing thing was, that company wasn't even in California. In fact, they're based on the east coast! It didn't matter to them, though. As long as he produced quality work, he could live anywhere.

The moral to Ryan and Kathryn's story is quite simple: By walking in obedience, leaving everything and everyone they knew in order to follow God, He provided what they didn't even know they needed.

The same is true for you, too.

He knows where you are, where you are going, and how to make everything work together. God's provision always goes ahead of you. When you follow, you're stepping into a series of miracles just waiting for your arrival.

HE'S PROVIDED EVERYTHING UP-FRONT!

"YOU WILL HAVE SUCH A SURPLUS OF CROPS THAT YOU WILL NEED TO CLEAR OUT THE OLD GRAIN TO MAKE ROOM FOR THE NEW HARVEST."

LEVITICUS 26:10
| New Living Translation |

That Always Happens to Me

One Sunday morning, Cyndy and I were listening to Dr. Jerry Savelle speak at Eagle Mountain International Church. During his message, he told how he came home from a trip, and the first letter he opened included a check for $100,000! Immediately, we looked at each other and said out loud, "THAT ALWAYS HAPPENS TO ME!"

Now, you might ask, "Well, how many $100,000 checks have *you* received?" The answer is, "They are still on the way!"

This may sound a bit unconventional, but think of the alternative. If we go around saying, "That never happens to me," guess what? It won't! So, now when something good happens, we say, "That always happens to me!" It builds our faith for more miracles, and we need all the miracles we can get!

Last Christmas we saw this in action.

Whenever we bought gift cards for Christmas presents, we received several bonus gift cards as a result. After Christmas, we determined to use these bonus gift cards to buy dinner for several friends. But each time, our friends insisted on paying the bill, leaving us with the gift cards.

One night after a photo shoot, we went out to eat, since we were all dressed up. At the end of our meal, our server said, "Your ticket has already been taken care of." When she left our table, Cyndy and I looked at each other and said: (Say it with me.)

"THAT ALWAYS HAPPENS TO ME!"

Practically every Christian has heard the name for God, Jehovah Jireh. Do you know what it means? It means, "The God who sees ahead and provides." God knows how, when, where, and through whom to manifest His infinite wisdom and miracle-working power on your behalf. The Bible says that He knows what you need before you even ask. (See Matthew 6:8.)

Get ready! The paid-up-front anointing is being released.

It's time to receive it because . . .

"THAT ALWAYS HAPPENS TO ME!"

Fillionaire

STRATEGIES

#9

. . . FOR THE PAID-UP-FRONT ANOINTING

* Prepare your heart to see paid-up-front provision.
* Meditate on God bringing you paid-up-front miracles.
* Change your words to line up with paid-up-front.
* Stop saying, "Bad things always happen to me!"
* Start saying, "Blessings always happen to me!"

DECLARE THESE:

"God already knew what I needed and it's paid up-front."

"These things dominate the thoughts of unbelievers, but your heavenly Father already knows your needs." (Matthew 6:32, NLT)

"God has stored up paid-up-front blessings for me!"

"How abundant are the good things that you have stored up for those who fear you." (Psalms 31:19, NIV)

"God has upfront provision and protection for me and my family."

"You prepare a feast before me in the presence of my enemies. You honor me by anointing my head with oil. My cup overflows with blessings." (Psalms 23:5, NLT)

"God has appointed paid-up-front people in my life!"

"Joseph then ordered his servants to fill the men's sacks with grain, but he also gave secret instructions to return each brother's payment at the top of his sack. He also gave them supplies for their journey home." (Genesis 42:25, NLT)

"Good things always happen to me!"

"If you come with us, we will share with you all the good things the LORD gives us." (Numbers 10:32, GW)

Living the Fillionaire Life

CHAPTER 10

STEP
| step |

TO SET, TO FIX; A PACE; ADVANCE; MOVEMENT MADE, GRADUATION OR DEGREE, PROGRESSION, ACTION

There's nothing like living the FILLIONAIRE life! The best part is, you can always add more—more of His presence, more of His glory, more miracles, more supernatural interventions, etc.

The FILLIONAIRE life is a life filled to overflowing—and then some!

As you mediate on the precepts and ideas presented in this book, my prayer is that God would open your eyes to see:

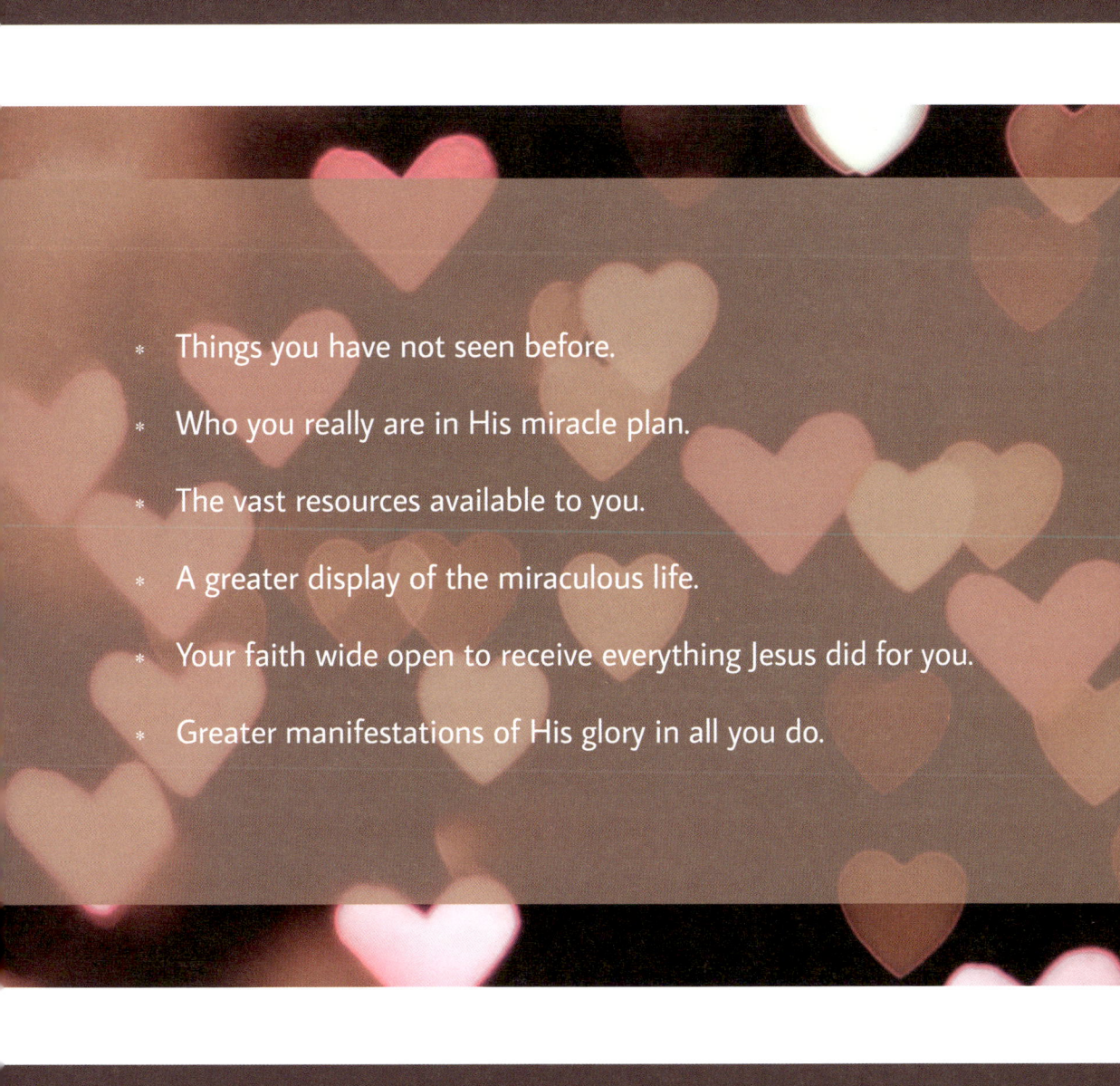

* Things you have not seen before.

* Who you really are in His miracle plan.

* The vast resources available to you.

* A greater display of the miraculous life.

* Your faith wide open to receive everything Jesus did for you.

* Greater manifestations of His glory in all you do.

Prayer to Pray

As you're walking and living the FILLIONAIRE life, moving up to a new level in God, keep your prayer life at the forefront. Here's a prayer for you to pray every day to significantly step into your destiny:

"Father, in the name of Jesus, You have expanded our vision. You have shown us; You have drawn out the map, God, and we see where it is going. We see what we need to do to prepare to go forward and move ahead.

Father, when we started, we couldn't see the map very clearly. Father, in Jesus' name, You have filled in all the streets and all the highways and all the roads to where we need to go. Thank You for the strength, the wisdom, the vision, the greatness, and the glory.

Thank You for imparting into us faith for the steps ahead. We release all our faith—all our faith to take this on. This is our great year! This is our great path! This is our great time! This is the plan, . . . the plan, ... the plan, . . . the plan.

So, Father, in the name of Jesus, as we step into the fulfill-ment of Your plan, we declare that it will be quicker than any-one thought. It will come together quicker than anyone ever anticipated. Father, in Jesus' name, we release all the pieces to come together.

I thank You for all the millionaires and billionaires rising up in the church to finance it.

I thank You for all the engineers to help build it, all the pilots, all the authors, and all the people You are raising up to make it all happen.

Father, in Jesus' name, we lift up the hands of our pastors, so that they have the supernatural strength and insight to take us there.

I thank You, God, that You are doing it; and You have done it. I call it accomplished!

Fulfillment is ours in Jesus' name.

Amen!"

"OUR HEARTS ARE NOT TURNED BACK, NEITHER HAVE OUR STEPS DECLINED FROM YOUR PATH."

PSALMS 44:18

| Amplified Bible Classic Edition |

A Prophetic Word for You

I want to close this book with a strong prophetic word I received from the Lord. I believe it illustrates the fullness of living the FILLIONAIRE life.

"'All of My glory, all of My goodness, all of My presence—My greatness is upon you now. My greatness has been released to you now. I have called you to walk in greatness, to step up into My level of greatness, so that you can step with Me and walk with Me. See Me working in all your affairs, in all your dealings, and in all you put your hand to do. For have I not said that in that day the sun will be darkened and the moon shall be turned into blood? That has happened. That has taken place in that great and awesome day of the Lord.

God is telling you that you have stepped into the Great Day of the Lord.

God is telling you that you have stepped into the greatness.

You have stepped into the new level.

You have stepped into the flow of GREAT! So, the Lord Your great God . . . the Lord Your great God . . . The Lord your great God has said, 'Come, walk with Me in greatness. Get ready for your great day! This is your great and awesome day! This is your great and awesome day!' says the Lord."

ABOUT THE AUTHORS

SPENCER & CYNDY NORDYKE are both dynamic speakers and anointed ministers with a strong prophetic perspective for the Body of Christ. They always have an encouraging word from God that will inspire vision and get people to use their faith

Their hearts are to minister to churches and their staffs, because they believe in the five-fold ministry and want to help build leadership teams throughout the world.

God sends them on specific assignments to pray over cities and areas to help change the spiritual atmosphere while declaring His Word. They go and listen to the Holy Spirit, pray, and deliver God's message to help make a difference in people's lives.

CONTACT

Nordyke Ministries
P O Box 1591
Hurst, TX 76053

| E-mail |
spencer@nordykeministries.com
cyndy@nordykeministries.com

| Website |
nordykeministries.com
spencernordyke.com

| Facebook |
/nordykeministries/

| Twitter |
@nordykeministry

| YouTube |
/nordykeministries

BIBLE TRANSLATIONS USED IN *FILLIONAIRE*

Scripture quotations marked (KJ21) are taken from *The Holy Bible, 21ˢᵗ Century King James Version.*® Copyright © 1994. Used by permission of Deuel Enterprises, Inc., Gary, SD 57237. All rights reserved.

Scripture quotations marked (ASV) are taken from the *American Standard Version.* This translation of the Bible is in the public domain.

Scripture quotations marked (AMPC) are taken from the *Amplified*® *Bible Classic Edition.* Copyright © 1954, 1958, 1962, 1964, 1965, 1987 by The Lockman Foundation. Used by permission. www.Lockman.org

Scripture quotations marked (BSB) are taken from *The Holy Bible, Berean Study Bible.* Copyright © 2016 by Bible Hub. All rights reserved worldwide.

Scripture quotations marked (CEV) are taken from the *Contemporary English Version.* Copyright © 1995 by the American Bible Society. All rights reserved.

Scripture quotations marked (DBY) are taken from the *Darby Translation.* This translation of the Bible is in the public domain.

Scripture quotations marked (ESV) are taken from *The Holy Bible, English Standard Version.* Copyright © 2001, 2007, 2011, 2016 by Crossway Bibles, a division of Good News Publishers. Used by permission. All rights reserved.

Scripture quotations marked (GW) are taken from *God's Word.*® Copyright © 1995 by God's Word to the Nations. Used by permission of Baker Publishing Group.

Scripture quotations marked (HCSB) are taken from the Holman Christian Standard Bible.® Copyright © 1999, 2000, 2002, 2003, 2009 by Holman Bible Publishers. Used with permission by Holman Bible Publishers; Nashville, TN. All rights reserved.

Scripture quotations marked (ISV) are taken from *The Holy Bible: International Standard Version.* Release 2.0, Build 2015.02.09. Copyright © 1995-2014 by ISV Foundation. All rights reserved internationally. Used by permission of Davidson Press, LLC.

Scripture quotations marked (JUB) are taken from *The Jubilee Bible* (from *The Scriptures of the Reformation*) edited by Russell M. Stendal. Copyright © 2000, 2001, 2010.